MY FIRST YEAR AS A TEACHER

EDITED BY
Pearl Rock Kane
Teachers College
Columbia University

Encouraged and supported by the
Geraldine R. Dodge Foundation
with assistance from *Education Week*

OUACHITA TECHNICAL COLLEGE
A SIGNET BOOK

SIGNET
Published by New American Library, a division of
Penguin Putnam Inc., 375 Hudson Street, New York, New York 10014, U.S.A.
Penguin Books Ltd, 80 Strand, London WC2R 0RL, England
Penguin Books Australia Ltd, 250 Camberwell Road, Camberwell, Victoria 3124,
Australia
Penguin Books Canada Ltd, 10 Alcorn Avenue, Toronto, Ontario, Canada M4V 3B2
Penguin Books (N.Z.) Ltd, 182–190 Wairau Road, Auckland 10, New Zealand

Penguin Books Ltd, Registered Offices: Harmondsworth, Middlesex, England

Published by Signet, an imprint of New American Library,
a division of Penguin Putnam Inc.
Previously published in a Mentor edition under the title *The First Year of
Teaching*.
Published by arrangement with Walker and Company. For information address
Walker and Company, 720 Fifth Avenue, New York, New York 10019.

First Mentor Printing, September 1992
First Signet Printing, July 1996
15 14 13 12

To my children Bradley, Laura, Leslie, and Lisa

And to the teachers who have made a
difference in their lives

Contents

*

Acknowledgments

*

This book is a result of the dedication of many teachers who care about young people and who care about the quality of teachers leading classrooms throughout the nation. Nearly four hundred teachers contributed their autobiographical stories for consideration for this book. Others, mostly teachers pursuing graduate study at Teachers College, Columbia University, where I am on the faculty, assisted in organizing the contest and judging the stories that were submitted. Loretta Sharp, Kinne Stires, and Carole DeVito worked with me in developing the conceptualization of the book and the notion of a contest as a way to collect authentic stories about the first year of teaching. A conversation with Richard Hawley steered us in the direction of focusing on beginning teachers.

The Geraldine R. Dodge Foundation and its wise and energetic executive director, Scott McVay, encouraged us and provided the needed financial support that made the contest possible. Ronald Wolk, the creative editor of *Education Week* and *Teacher Magazine*, generously provided supplementary awards of subscriptions to those leading educational journals. Betty Lies, Joan Countryman, Marty Bien, and Peter Herzberg helped to organize the contest and promote it among various groups of teachers. Camilla Vitullo did the publicity with the assistance of Roy Campbell.

None of us anticipated the enormous response that the contest elicited. The nearly four hundred stories we received exceeded any of our expectations. It was a delightful surprise, but it made coordinating the selection of the award winners a difficult and time-consuming task that Abner Oakes and Rob Rauh undertook with great skill and thoughtfulness. Nancy Kroonenberg, Robert Kirk, David Estrada, Suellen Newman, Joan Glazebrook, Michael Barrett, Alexander Wilkie, Nancy Spencer, Douglas Neuman, James Blitch, and Sarah Gillman, along with many of the people already mentioned, assisted in the selection process, carefully reading and commenting on each story to help determine the winners. Those teachers also provided advice on which stories should be included in the final collection. Jane Mallison assisted with the editing and made excellent suggestions on the final draft. Delma Lopez helped to organize the final stages of the manuscript and our review of the page proofs.

What kept us motivated throughout this long process were the nearly four hundred teachers who shared their heartfelt stories. They inspired us in our work as teachers and sustained our interest in the production of this book. I owe personal thanks to my husband, Richard, for his enduring support and helpful criticism and to my children for their enthusiasm for my work.

Foreword

*

Only a dramatic restructuring of the American education system will solve the problems in our schools. That restructuring will not come from an infusion of public dollars but from an infusion of the creativity and energy of human capital. Recruiting highly qualified teachers who are motivated to make a difference is a first priority in improving schooling.

In my own efforts to recruit teachers, I must have introduced myself to thousands of people during the summer following my graduation from college. I enthusiastically told school district officials, corporate and foundation leaders, and champions of educational reform: "I just graduated from Princeton and I'm creating a national teachers corps." I told them I was going to recruit five hundred of the nation's outstanding college seniors to commit two years to teaching in urban and rural schools experiencing chronic and sometimes desperate teacher shortages. These recruits would be campus leaders with strong academic backgrounds, who would choose to teach despite numerous other career opportunities.

Few believed it was possible to assemble such a teaching corps. Many insisted that people who could be lawyers or doctors or who could earn $50,000 a year in other fields *would not teach*. But I knew many would try teaching if given a chance.

In the fall of my senior year I was wandering around Princeton completely uninspired by the job hunt and desperately searching for a senior thesis topic. Many of my friends were seeking jobs in investment banking not because of a commitment to high finance or even because of the high salaries, but because working on Wall Street is perceived as a high-prestige, short-term commitment; some of them planned to stay for only two years and then move on to something more meaningful. But what many of them did, of course, was become committed to high finance. What kept coming back to me was the idea of a two-year commitment.

An unusual opportunity presented itself that fall. I attended a conference of business, education, and government leaders brought together with students from all over the country. These "leaders of today and tomorrow" had an admirable goal: to develop action plans to improve the education system. What struck me at the conference was that—as speaker after speaker deplored the sorry state of the schools and described, among other things, the difficulty school systems have attracting good teachers—surprisingly, a number of students in attendance expressed a real interest in teaching.

The enthusiasm of those students at the conference got me thinking long and hard about the problem of recruiting teachers. Why not create an aura of selectivity and service and status around teaching as a career,

I wondered? Why not make teaching a possibility for all college graduates, and not just education majors? Why not offer a short-term commitment as an option? There had to be a way to allow college students to keep their options open while committing themselves to teach for, say, two years. Many of the brightest graduates understandably want employment that lets them take responsibility right away, and they also want something that makes a genuine difference in society. What better way than by becoming a part of a national corps of teachers dedicated to doing the best possible job with their students, and at the same time working toward an educational system that provides all children an equal opportunity?

As my senior year progressed, I became obsessed with the concept of a teacher corps, and it became the focus of my senior thesis. Later, spurred on by the White House's negative response to my suggestion that the president launch the teacher corps as a federal program, I decided to create a teacher corps as a privately funded nonprofit organization.

With seed money from a corporation, I was able to assemble a dynamic, dedicated group of recent graduates and in a few months we created Teach for America. We recruited actively at one hundred colleges and universities, eliciting over 2,500 applications in the first year. We sought candidates who demonstrated commitment and flexibility, leadership potential and professionalism, who expressed high expectations for all students, and demonstrated sensitivity to diversity of student backgrounds and learning styles.

The five hundred charter "corps members" selected for the first Teach for America cohort participated in an eight-week institute to introduce them to theoretical understandings and basic teaching techniques. Individuals from this initial group are now teaching in New York, Los Angeles, New Orleans, Baton Rouge, and rural Georgia and North Carolina. Corps members tell us that teaching is the toughest, most challenging, frustrating, stressful, and rewarding experience they have ever had. It pushes them to their limits, and leads them to ask tough questions: Why are students turned off to learning? How can schools compensate for the failure of other social institutions? Why are there inequities in the resource allocation in schools? And how, despite these impediments, are some teachers able to make such a big difference in their students' lives?

This book provides interesting answers to such questions. The stories here, written by teachers across the country reflecting on their first year in the classroom, vividly describe the challenges and rewards of teaching. *My First Year as a Teacher* will be interesting reading for those new to teaching or for those deciding whether to teach. The stories reveal that unlike most jobs, teaching offers young people an opportunity to assume significant responsibility and to have an impact on society.

—Wendy Kopp,
founder and director,
Teach for America, Inc.

Introduction

*

If you are thinking of becoming a teacher, or if you are experiencing your first year of teaching, or enjoy remembering that first year, this book is for you.

To the observer, teaching may look easy. Years of watching good and bad teaching as a student may provide the uninitiated with a notion of what works in the classroom and what should be avoided. But being a passenger is hardly the same as steering. The ride in a jet may be smooth or bumpy, but the passengers may not know whether to attribute the result to the weather conditions or to the skill of the captain. Teaching offers its own set of challenges because the path is often uncharted and there is no control tower to provide guidance in the midst of an unforeseen situation.

This book attempts to reveal what teaching entails in ways that are seldom accessible to the observer. The stories in this volume, all of them true, are vivid personal accounts of the first year of teaching. The stories were written for a nationwide contest called "In the

Beginning." Teachers were invited to write their personal accounts of the trying and triumphant moments, the pivotal decisions, the humorous or awkward situations, the lessons they had taught and learned during their first year of teaching. Nearly four hundred stories were submitted; many arrived with accompanying notes of appreciation for the opportunity to tell beginning teachers what the authors wish they had known at that stage of their careers.

A panel of teachers read each of the stories that were submitted and submitted the finalists to a committee of educational leaders from across the country. The committee included Albert Shanker, president of the American Federation of Teachers; Mary Furtrell, former president of the National Education Association and currently associate director of the Center for the Study of Education at George Washington University; Ernest Boyer, president of the Carnegie Foundation for the Advancement of Teaching; Scott McVay, executive director of the Geraldine R. Dodge Foundation; Thomas Kean, president of Drew University and former governor of New Jersey; and Ronald Wolk, editor of *Education Week* and *Teacher Magazine*. Authors of the sixty stories ranked in the top categories received awards. The stories selected for this volume are those considered not only the most poignant and lively but also the most useful for conveying the realities of the classroom during that first year—the fears, the joys, the disappointments, the satisfactions, and the challenges.

Collectively, these stories reveal that the challenges and difficulties of teaching may also be the factors that make it appealing, particularly to young men and women who are eager to make a difference in the lives of others and to test their own abilities. In almost any other kind of work open to recent college graduates, new employees are given limited duties the first year on the job. It takes months, sometimes years, before neophytes are considered sufficiently seasoned to handle increased responsibility or to make the kind of independent decisions that teachers must make the first day on the job. Indeed, few other jobs offer the immediate challenge, the magnitude of responsibility, or the potential for intrinsic satisfaction and learning that teaching in an elementary or secondary school affords from the first day of employment.

As David Callaway reveals in his story, "Ever Been to Disneyland?" even the first hour of that first day can be daunting:

Once I separated the pugilists, intercepted the rugby ball, and suggested that everyone find a seat, the general riot simmered to a reasonable calm. The stage was mine. The rambunctious twelve-year-olds waited for my next move. And so did I.

Many teachers quickly discover that they have very different goals from those of their students, as Marcia Nehemiah describes in her story, "The Road."

I wanted to make literature come alive. I wanted to instill a love of the written word. I wanted to discuss F. Scott Fitzgerald's use of metaphor in *The Great Gatsby*. They wanted to throw spitballs and whisper dirty words in the back of the room.

Unlike other professions, where the toughest cases are usually reserved for the most adept and experienced, beginning teachers are often given the most difficult assignments. Janice Connolly's class of failing students who labeled themselves "retards" is an example of an unreasonable assignment for a young teacher; at the same time it also demonstrates that a determined teacher, even a first-year one, has the potential to overcome the odds. Connolly makes the advice she received—"Don't waste your time with those kids"—the title of her story; her sense that the advice was wrong helped her find a way to restore her students' self-esteem and motivate them to learn.

In many situations, teachers must adjust not only to a new job but also to an unfamiliar culture. Teachers may find themselves teaching students whose backgrounds and ways of life bear little resemblance to their own. In "The University School," Emma Lewinsohn describes her first experience in teaching in one of the poorest cities in the Northeast, an experience that served to enlarge her understanding of life situations dramatically different from her own:

From them I learned what it is like to grow up with immigrant parents, divorced parents, alcoholic parents, or no parents. Unlike me or my fellow students in college, they did not take for granted a college education, a nine-to-five office job, a suburban home, or a happy family.

Challenges of entering an unfamiliar culture may be compounded when teachers attempt to help students whose lives are overwhelmed by daily stress and grief. Nancy Gustafson's story, "David," which takes place in rural Kentucky, shows how an untenable family situation impedes learning and can rob a child of happiness, but it also reveals how absorbed teachers can become in their students' lives.

Many stories tell about individual students who were particularly disruptive or particularly troubling, the "difficult cases" that teachers take home with them and think about at the end of the day, long after they lock the classroom door. Kayla McClurg's story about the transformation of incorrigible Leo provides a shining example. Leo was spending his third year in the eighth grade, a fact that gave him two years of seniority over his rookie teacher. His enthusiasm for coming to school was surpassed only by his relentless antics, including turning a pig loose in the school. But Leo's life was turned around in that eighth-grade class by the teacher's ability to elicit group support, and, in the process, his teacher's life was also changed.

Among the difficult cases that teachers find most troubling are students who are hauntingly silent, potentially the signal of a deeply rooted problem. The unfolding mystery in Rosemary DiBattista's story, "Adrianna," not only exemplifies how a teacher may change the course of a student's life but also how teachers learn through reflection. DiBattista asks, "What had I done for her? I didn't know then, but now I think that she looked at me and saw someone she could be."

Just as DiBattista's story shows how Adrianna changed her way of viewing herself as a teacher, so too do numerous stories submitted for the "In the Beginning" contest show that the experiences of the first year of teaching may shape a teacher's practice or even a teacher's career. The lessons learned from experience, as the old adage suggests, appear to leave a particularly indelible impression during that first year. In "Answers and Questions," Z. Vance Wilson confesses that his students got more involved and the classroom discussions about literature became more engaging when he learned to stop answering his own questions. On the advice of a fellow teacher, Wilson began to practice silent counting for six seconds rather than giving in to an almost irresistible urge to supply an instant answer himself.

In "Learning to Read," English teacher Patrick McWilliams tells how Laurie, a student in his first-year writing class, taught him the difference between being a critic and being a teacher. McWilliams says he had thought his job was to find the faults in his students' writing until Laurie looked at him one day with the same puffed-out cheeks she had when giving a swift kick to a soccer ball and said, "How would you feel if someone asked you to write about something you cared deeply about, and then they write 'cliché, cliché, cliché' in the margin after every other sentence?"

Other teachers learned how close interaction between student and material caused more learning to occur. In his first year, Andrew Mullen's fourth-grade class was going smoothly, but he discovered he was the one working the hardest, doing the most, and enjoying it less each day. The result was a growing resentment of his students: "How dare they just sit there and not fully appreciate everything I was doing for them?" In "Order in the Classroom," Mullen learned that students like doing more of the work of running the classroom, and that such increased involvement also leads to more learning. Similarly, in "Death in the Classroom," Judy Luster tells about a risk she took with her Contemporary World Drama class when she asked the students to relate the theme of grief in Maeterlinck's play *Interior* to grief in their own lives. "The room had been full of death," Luster says, and she admits that had she known that fact she would have been too frightened to assign the play. "It makes me wonder how many doors we've helped to close in the classroom rather than encouraged to open. It makes me remember to take risks."

When teachers must rely on their own ingenuity, they often invent creative solutions to problems. In her story, Anita Charles describes the method she devised to quiet incorrigible first grader Carla. Charles gave her a pad of paper and told her to draw a picture or write something down whenever she felt like saying something at a time that was unacceptable or inappropriate. The approach appeared to work. One day Carla showed her pad of paper to the teacher. "It say, I'm very mad at you, Ms. Anita." Charles nodded solemnly and said, "I see," and Carla, overjoyed with her own success in communication, hugged the teacher and grinned.

In the middle of her rookie year, Julie Olin Schulz was introduced to Sonny, a new student for her first-grade class. When Sonny cheerily greeted her with, "Hi, baby doll! How ya doin'?" she knew something was awry. Later Schulz discovered that Sonny had recently been the victim of an accident that left him disfigured and caused him to have social and verbal responses that were often inappropriate and sexually explicit. Schulz grew fond of Sonny, but she made little progress in teaching him to read. In May, when the class began to practice for the big event of reading an entire book out loud to their "little buddy" in a kindergarten class, Sonny wanted to read, too. Schulz solved the problem by finding a picture book and asking Sonny to make up a story to go with the pictures. She then typed his story into the book, thus allowing Sonny to have the pleasure and feeling of accomplishment of "reading" his known-by-heart story to a younger student.

Sometimes the inventiveness of a new teacher can take the wrong direction. In "Johnny Carson Was My Mentor," Latin teacher Ronald Thorpe describes the way he studied the monologue at the beginning of *The Tonight Show* on television to develop a stand-up comic style of teaching, which seemed to hold the attention of his students. Thorpe laments the amount of time it took him to discover the crucial difference between teaching and entertaining.

Numerous stories show that beginning teachers devise ingenious ways to solve problems by being resourceful and flexible and trying different approaches; when, however, important moral issues are involved, the teachers are resolute about what needs to be done. In "Plagiarism," Ted Fitts demonstrates that he is unwilling to make ethical compromises even in the face of an angry lawyer/father whose son has plagiarized parts of a term paper. In "The Forest and the Tree," Elizabeth Esris reports on how she dealt with eighth graders in a class where there had been repeated incidents of theft and vandalism. In "The Ultimate Challenge," Polly Rimer Duke describes how she handled questions of racial prejudice in a boarding school dormitory. Duke says that her first year taught her this: "Laugh a lot at yourself, admit your many weaknesses, but hold on to your convictions."

Sometimes, sad to say, the problems teachers confront are other teachers. In his story of a memorable first year, Brad Wilcox tells about the suspicion he confronted as an enthusiastic young male teacher in an elementary school. Wilcox found a way to break through the hostility, and his sustained enthusiasm for teaching, which at first had perturbed some senior colleagues, spilled over and influenced their behavior.

One of the greatest advantages of teaching over other types of employment is its forgiving quality. Children may be more tolerant of errors than adults, and a blunder in teaching one day can be rectified the next. The classroom offers potential for change and growth for students and teachers alike. There are numerous possibilities for redemption as David Gould says in "You Can't."

A teacher can have a terrific day and a horrible day within the same day, sometimes within the same forty-two-minute period. The lesson that failed miserably in the first period can work beautifully an hour later. The student you loathe one day can say something thoughtful and memorable the next.

And teachers must balance multiple goals. Albert Thompson found a letter of advice that he had written in 1935 to a boyhood friend who was about to begin his first year as a teacher. In "A Letter to Luke," Thompson's advice about the need to juggle a number of goals has a timeless quality. Teachers have to encourage students' autonomy while also training them to work in a group.

To be polite, to have good social attitudes, to be a good citizen, to be prepared to take a rightful place in the world, to work with others and yet have independent views, to conform to the silly little disciplinary rules you must perforce set up and yet be ready to aid in reforming the future world he or she must live in. . . . O teacher, how manifold are thy works!

Many teachers revel in exactly the diversity and complexity that Thompson delineates. Inherent in teaching is the challenge of making the class interesting and meaningful while meeting the varying needs of individual students. In "The Accidental Teacher," Katherine Schulten describes the joy of that intensity:

> The people who graduated from college with me all have jobs in offices in Manhattan and Boston and Philadelphia. They talk about watching the clock and living for weekends. I live for weekdays. When I'm in school, I'm completely absorbed.
>   The things you can think about during the day while you're teaching are some of the most engaging things there are.

Some of the stories are written by men and women who gave up more lucrative careers to enter teaching. In his story, "The Green Monongahela," John Taylor Gatto tells why he left his work as a copywriter on "the fast track" at an advertising agency in order to teach in a junior high school. Gatto had been successful at writing thirty-second television commercials, and he spent much of his time in power breakfasts and with after-work martinis.

> It bothered me that all the urgencies of the job were generated externally, but it bothered me more that the work I was doing seemed to have very little importance—even to the people who were paying for it.

Although the authors speak of many satisfactions in their work, few of the stories submitted to "In the Beginning" have fairy-tale endings. Authors are honest in conveying the truth that teaching young people is a highly complex task. The leitmotiv running through these stories is that the first year of teaching challenges the personal and intellectual skills of an individual to the fullest. This truth seems to hold in public, private, and parochial schools; in inner cities, suburbs, or affluent boarding schools; in kindergarten or in twelfth grade.

With all the tension and pressure of such a challenge, is teaching worth it? The answer from those who submitted entries for this book is a clear yes. Some teachers, like Yetta Farber, had planned only a brief stint in teaching but got "hooked." Farber had intended to teach for only one year before entering medical school. In "My Ambition: To Teach," she discloses that what kept her in teaching was a feeling of being desperately needed. Farber was teaching in one of the poorest sections of Brooklyn, New York, in a school where classes were too large, equipment was poor, and supplies were meager. For Farber, the feeling of filling a need was so powerful that she decided not to become a pediatrician; nonetheless, she became a healer of children—a teacher. For others who stay in teaching, the decision is marked by more ambivalence. In his story, "Graduation," Ron Wolfson describes his first year of teaching in a high school class labeled "slow learners," where students were destructive, rude, immature, and often uncontrollable. Yet observing them at a graduation ceremony, he notes that he found their graduation more meaningful to him than his own. He knows, he says, that he will continue to live with uncertainties but that "the equation of effort to results, of positives to negatives, while never properly balanced, could still tilt just far enough toward satisfying to make teaching worthwhile."

The first year of teaching may turn out to be as memorable for students as it is for teachers. Twenty-five years after teaching her first class of fourth graders, Roberta Sherman received an invitation for dinner from former students Mark, Steven, and Mitchell. She was picked up in a limousine and toasted with champagne. After dinner her former students gave her a solar-powered calculator with the inscription "Teacher of the Century—Miss Sherman."

For all teachers and potential teachers, our nation must continue to work to improve the external factors that are important in the career choices of talented young men and women. (An occasional champagne toast is delightful but not enough!) Although salaries still lag significantly behind those offered by other professions, the good news is that they are on the rise. Similarly, more schools are beginning to recognize the need to give teachers a larger say in the making of decisions of curriculum and policy that directly influence a teacher's effectiveness in the classroom.

It is imperative that more people be drawn to the classroom. Statistical studies show us that over the next five years the United States will need more than a million new teachers. A third of all teachers currently in the work force are age forty-five and over and will be retiring in the next fifteen years. At current rates only 135,000 people—roughly 65 percent of the number needed—are being trained each year. In the next decade, America will need large numbers of highly qualified teachers to meet the challenges of educating students to live in an increasingly poor and ethnically diverse society, and to help to solve the problems posed by such a society.

Providing salaries that more fully reflect the complexities of teaching and the importance of its role in a democracy and giving teachers a larger say in the governance of schools will help to attract more people into the teaching force. And yet, to a large degree, the intrinsic satisfactions of teaching may continue to be the most important factor in drawing talented and compassionate people to become teachers. By giving readers a vivid picture of their first-year classrooms, the authors of this volume invite intelligent and resourceful young men and women to picture themselves with a classroom of their own. The authors suggest that the experience will not be lacking in complications, stress, or even sadness, but they also make the implicit promise that the effort is worthwhile. I join these authors in hoping these stories may spark an interest in teaching in those who enjoy rising to meet a challenge, those who long for an inner life of their own, and those who want to make a difference, large or small, in the lives of others.

CHAPTER 1

"Ever Been to Disneyland?"

✳

David Callaway

"Where should we sit, sir?" asked a bright-eyed young fellow, his cowlick temporarily tamed by a severe, moist brushing. In the narrow doorway behind him bunched twenty-five other first formers, their cordovans shined, and their white shirts sharply pressed.

"Anywhere. It doesn't really matter, does it?" I answered.

As if I had just dragged open the gates to the Bastille, the mob poured past me into the classroom. Minutes before, the uniformed troops had stood in the eucalyptus-shaded courtyard, erect and at attention. Now they swarmed across chairs and tables like cannibals, or ants, over a fallen missionary. Desk tops slammed, fistfights erupted, and a rugby ball spiraled dangerously near the streetside windows.

At that moment Brother Dowding, the headmaster and an ex-army major, strode by on his way to the office. "Go get 'em, Dave. Remember, firm control is what they need," he said brightly, and with a meaty

14

hand guided me into the melee and closed the door behind me. My first class at the parochial school in Sydney, Australia, and my premiere appearance as a teacher were under way.

In the fall of that year, determined to see the world, I had applied for a visa, stuffed a backpack, and flown to Luxembourg. I trekked east from Istanbul to Jakarta and ended up in Sydney washing dishes. I had no intention of making a commitment to Australia, but my thinking changed when I read about a teaching position at a Catholic school there, run by an order of brothers. Fortunately for me, the school was about to open and valued enthusiasm over experience. I was hired, without a teaching certificate, three days before the fall term.

But the first day, the first hour, did not go as I had envisioned. Once I separated the pugilists, intercepted the rugby ball, and suggested that everyone find a seat, the general riot simmered to a reasonable calm. The stage was mine. The rambunctious twelve-year-olds waited for my next move. And so did I.

I picked up the class roll, the only bit of information I'd received about my charges, cleared my throat, and began. "Listen, when I call your name, please raise your hand."

"I can't hear you," crooned a voice from the rear of the class.

"I said, when you hear your name . . ." I paused. Six or seven separate conversations, like brushfires, now raged around the room. It was time, as Brother Dowding had implied, to take charge.

"I want it quiet—*now!*" I shouted. A stunned silence, like a settling cloud of dust, followed. Boys twisted around in their seats. A few sat upright. The chatter ceased. "I have to check your names," I explained, embarrassed at my outburst but nonetheless pleased with the results.

I read off the class list, stumbling over surnames as though I were reading Greek with a paper clip latched to my tongue. "That's Acqunaldo, sir. Ack. Ack. Ever since we come from the Philippines, no one says it right," moaned Joseph after I botched his name twice. I apologized and moved on. By the time I finished, I felt as if I had introduced the UN Security Council. Along with Acqunaldo there were Tony Biviano, Shane Summerville, Franco Spinoza, David Mailey, Joe Scandura, and an assortment of young fellows fresh from the shores of Greece and Lebanon.

"Aren't you forgetting something, sir?" called out Scandura, a wiry dark-haired kid with a pack of Winstons peeking from his shirt pocket.

"Uh, what?" My mind had fogged over completely. The sweat under my arms dripped to my waist.

"Your name."

"Oh, right." I turned and began to print my name on the board. The chalk snapped. An explosion of laughter followed.

"You're from the States, aren't you?" Scandura asked before I had finished my autograph. "Ever been to Disneyland?"

"Yeah, lots of times. In fact I lived less than an hour from there," I answered, wondering why I was falling under this interrogator's spell.

"What's it like?" asked Joe. This time the acid was out of his voice. The others in the class leaned forward, entranced, like Joe, by the mere mention of the Magic Kingdom.

"Well, Disneyland is divided up into different sections. There's Frontierland and . . ." I paused. I could hear the clock ticking. "Listen, if we get through our work today, I'll tell you all about Disneyland. But first . . ."

There was a general moan, but the class conceded they had been outmaneuvered. As the day progressed, I passed out the outdated English anthologies and examined my social studies program, a collection of musty dittos. When the general classroom hum grew to a crescendo and I felt an insurrection imminent, I had only to mention Disneyland and peace was restored. But there was never a time I felt in control. I always expected Scandura to strut to the front of the room, snatch the chalk from my hand, and expose me as an impostor.

In the adjoining room all was silence. Brother Gerard, fresh out of teachers' college, was in charge of the other first form. I thought he was alone when I poked my head in during my first free period. But his class was filled with twenty-five industrious students. A stack of math worksheets sat on each desk. Every boy scratched through one after another in complete silence. Brother Gerard, his arms folded across his chest, rocked confidently on his heels at the back of the still room. I slipped out. His boys scribbled on.

"Discipline is something personal, something you have to establish for yourself," explained Barry Kelley, another of the lay teachers. "What works for me or the Brothers might not be for you." The Brothers believed in a philosophy of right or wrong. No ambiguities were tolerated. If a student stepped out of line, he was punished, usually with the strap. This foot-long, half-inch leather belt was applied with vigor across the open palm. For minor infractions one crack was sufficient, but for major crimes such as fighting and cheating, boys were marched to the office and received "six of the best" from Brother Dowding. I struggled with the strap. The boys, especially Scandura, mocked me when I tapped gingerly and threatened me when a wrist was nicked. I abandoned the weapon altogether after my battle with David.

The tallest and oldest kid in the class, David, nick-named Mailbox by his classmates, suffered through life with a harelip and a partially repaired cleft palate. He spoke through his nose, hated school, and remains in my memory as the most stubborn child I have ever taught. David's favorite distraction was to squawk and bark into his hands when class became dull. Initially I humored him, but at the end of my second week I was through being considerate. I warned him once, and then twice, to quiet down. He answered with an enormous sheep bleat.

"Okay, David, up here," I said, reaching into my desk for the strap.

"No way. I didn't do nothing," he answered before he yanked himself from his desk, circled the room, and bolted out the door with me in pursuit. I collared him on the veranda of the Brothers' dormitory and slammed his shoulders against the building.

"What do you think you're doing?" I screamed.

"I just don't want to get hit. I ain't opening my hand. For nobody!" David was breathing hard, snorting out his words, gasping for air. We struck a quick bargain. If he kept the barnyard imitations out of class, I'd turn in my strap.

Without the strap open riot became a daily threat. And lacking any sort of curriculum guide, I agonized over the mystery of course planning. I envied the experienced teachers who strolled in each morning, sipped their coffee, adjusted their overhead projectors, and listened to classical music, while I frantically rehearsed lessons I'd whipped up the night before.

But gradually there were successes. I canned the social studies dittos for my personal passion, geography. The boys drew the routes they took to school, traced maps of European countries from the library's lone set of encyclopedias, and formed papier-mâché globes. The literature anthologies were discarded after I unearthed a dog-eared set of Jack Schaefer's wonderful novel *Shane*. Barry suggested *English through Poetry Writing* by Brian Powell, and in no time my international crew was knocking out Dylan Thomas imitations, couplets, haikus, and rough-cut sonnets. I began reading to the boys, and when we finished *The Cay* by Ted Taylor, little Mario, and then every boy in the class wrote the author. Mr. Taylor graciously responded with handwritten notes for each student, which were cradled on the homeward buses like sacred icons.

It was on Wednesday afternoons, sports day at school, that the boys taught me. In the ovals around the school, Shane explained the intricacies of cricket and Tony pitched me rugby balls, freshly popped from a scrum. I spotted strengths in boys who stumbled through their lessons. On Wednesdays, Franco, a gliding, gifted soccer player who couldn't multiply beyond five, cut and jagged through fourth-form teams as if they were cemented to the turf. I was in awe. My appreciation of his field prowess tempered my thoughts about his academic inabilities.

I also led expeditions to other schools on sports days. Once I shepherded a soccer team across Sydney Harbor while waves washed over the sides of a rolling ferry.

On the return cruise I hauled in two young athletes, tiptoeing along the railing, their shirttails flapping a few feet above the whitecaps. "Don't worry, sir," said one of the boys. "Brother Dowding says Wednesdays are a time for sportsmanship and daring." And heart attacks for rookie instructors.

The final day of the year, the boys really cut loose, and so did I. After scrubbing the room for Brother Dowding's final inspection, we loosened our ties, propped our feet on the desks, and guzzled orange sodas. David snuck a crumpled map of Australia, one he had drawn, up to my desk. "This is for you," he said. "So you don't forget where you are." Tony, the class captain, led the group in a rousing three cheers for Mr. C., and I capped off the festivities by sketching a detailed chalk outline of Disneyland. At three o'clock the boys blasted out the door for the last time.

I lack the long, perfect memory of some veteran teachers, but even today, fifteen years, three schools, and half a world away, what comes most vividly to mind are the faces of those first-year boys: Tony's cowlick, David's poor, misshapen jaw, and even Scandura's shifty smile. I remember them, nearly every one, and wonder at times if they ever think of the "Yank teacher" and the year we shared.

David Callaway has continued his teaching career, inspired by his first teaching job in Australia. He is now a member of the faculty of a middle school in New Hampshire.

CHAPTER 2

The Road

*

Marcia Nehemiah

My foot hesitated over the accelerator pedal of my $300 used 1969 Pontiac Bonneville. I checked my rearview mirror. The man in the car behind me shook his fist at my refusal to travel more than thirty-five miles an hour on this winding, hilly, country back road. How could I drive any faster without threatening the life of a horse that grazed placidly along the side of the road or side-swiping a tractor parked in a hay field?

I drove slowly on, leading a growing line of cars, the one immediately behind futilely attempting to pass me. I was definitely out of my element. But it was 1974, the job market was glutted with teachers, and after filling out fifty applications, trekking to four interviews, and winning one job offer, I had taken what I could get—a teaching job at what I considered a distant outpost of civilization: western New Jersey. My characteristic optimism prevailed only when I reminded myself that I would be doing what I had wanted to do since I was fourteen—teaching English.

The beginning days of September unfolded, and though I gradually mustered more boldness on the road, I felt more and more as if I were in foreign territory. Was this rural area really New Jersey? My students took a week off when hunting season began. I was told they were also frequently absent during dry spells in May to help their fathers make hay on the surrounding farms. I was a young woman from the developed suburbs of New York City, who thought that "Make hay while the sun shines" just meant to have a good time. When one of my students pointed to my Star of David and asked, "What's that?" I knew that this school in rural New Jersey was far removed from my hometown suburb, where at least half of my friends were Jewish.

But, still, I was teaching English. I was proud, exhilarated, challenged. I worked a long day, taking time off only to eat and sleep. Every day was a new adventure: I delved into the pages of *Macbeth* and wracked my brains for provocative questions about *Silas Marner*. On a more mundane level, I stumbled through the proper procedures for filling out an attendance sheet and forgot to put my blinds halfway down at the end of the day, thus earning a reprimanding letter from the principal for my permanent file.

And then there was my sixth-period class—seventeen boys and five girls who were only six years younger than I. I had a problem long before I knew it. I was struggling in my work as only a young idealistic teacher can. I wanted to make literature come alive. I wanted to instill a love of the written word. I wanted to discuss F. Scott Fitzgerald's use of metaphor in *The Great Gatsby*. They wanted to throw spitballs and whisper dirty words in the back of the room.

In college I had learned from my educational psychology text that a successful educator should ignore bad behavior. So I did, smugly confident that, as the book had said, the bad behavior would disappear as I gave my students positive attention. It sounds rational, but the text apparently ignored the fact that humans, particularly adolescents, rarely seem rational. During that first year, by the time my department chairman came into the classroom to observe me, the students exhibited very little good behavior to praise. As a teacher, I was beyond wilting: I was withered and buried.

During my first observation session, my taskmaster sat in the back of the room. This man had a reputation among the faculty as the harshest, most demanding, most quick to fire inexperienced teachers that anyone had ever seen. The boys in the class were making animal noises, giggling, punching each other while the girls filed their nails or read *Seventeen* magazine. At least their talk about the new winter fashions was carried on only in whispers. I pretended it all wasn't happening.

I went on lecturing and tried to ask questions about the short story "Haircut." My boss, sitting in the back of the room, seemed to be growing bigger and bigger. After twenty minutes he left, silently. I should have been glad that he was gone, but his leaving seemed like a sign of disaster. Visions of unemployment marched before my eyes.

I felt mildly triumphant that I got through the rest of class without crying, but I felt like a puddle of melting slush. At my next free period I had to face him. I wondered if he would let me finish out the day. I walked to his closet of an office, took a deep breath, and opened the door.

He was sitting in his chair, and he looked at me long and hard. I said nothing. All I could think of was that I was not an English teacher; I had been lying to myself, pretending that everything was fine.

When he spoke, he said simply, without accusation, "You had nothing to say to them."

This felt unfair to me. I was a Phi Beta Kappa!

"You had nothing to say to them," he repeated. "No wonder they're bored. Why not get to the meat of the literature and stop talking about symbolism. Talk with them, not at them. And, more important, why do you ignore their bad behavior?" A brief impulse to refer to Ed Psych 101 crossed my mind, but I knew he was right. I knew my disciplinary tactics had failed and that my teaching had therefore failed.

We talked. He named my problems and offered solutions. We role-played. He was the bad student, and I was the forceful, yet warm, teacher. As the year progressed, we spent many hours discussing literature and ideas about human beings and their motivations. He helped me identify my weaknesses and my strengths. In short, he made a teacher of me by teaching me the reality of Ralph Waldo Emerson's words, "The secret to education lies in respecting the pupil."

Fifteen years later I still drive that same winding road to school, but it isn't perilous to me anymore. Much to my dismay I got my first speeding ticket a few months ago. I lost track of my speed as I was thinking about the vibrant student-led discussion on an Emily Dickinson poem in my ninth-period class. We were struggling to understand the poem when suddenly light bulbs lit about our twenty-three heads. We all laughed together at the delight of shared comprehension.

The school is my home now, where I share life with a group of young adults that changes every year. I do have something to say to them, thanks to the help I received that difficult first year. I also listen to what they have to say to me and learn from it. We share the joy, struggle, reward, and purpose of learning together. And each year I post Emerson's quotation on my bulletin board as a message to my students and a reminder to myself.

Marcia Nehemiah teaches at a high school in New Jersey, where she began her teaching career seventeen years ago.

CHAPTER 3

"Don't Waste Your Time with Those Kids"

*

Janice Anderson Connolly

On my first day of teaching all my classes were going well. The kids had taken notes eagerly, the bright faces had looked at me in the seemingly appropriate way, and I had decided that being a teacher was going to be a cinch. The last class of the day, however, broke all the rules and made me realize how sterile and packaged my earlier presentations had been.

Long before I entered the room, I had known there was trouble. I heard a piece of furniture crash against the wall, and as I rounded the corner I saw one boy pinning another to the floor.

"Listen, you retard!" yelled the one on the bottom. "I don't give a damn about your sister!"

"You keep your hands off her, you hear?" the boy on top threatened.

I drew up my short frame, and in my best teacherly manner I asked them to stop their fighting.

Suddenly, fourteen pairs of eyes were riveted on my face. I knew I did not look convincing. Glaring at each other and at me, the two boys slowly took their seats. At that moment, a teacher from a classroom across the hall stuck his head in the door and shouted at my class.

He had taught many of these same students in summer school, as I later learned. He was now telling them to sit down, shut up, and do what Miss Anderson said or they'd be sorry. He returned to his classroom, and I was left, feeling more than a little powerless, in what appeared to be a demilitarized zone.

I tried to repeat my morning lessons in which I had taken such pride, but I was met with a sea of guarded faces. As the class was leaving, I detained Mark, the boy who had seemed to be the instigator of the fight. With a dead voice he said to me, "Lady, don't waste your time. We're the retards." Dumbstruck, I didn't respond, and he strolled out of the room.

I slumped into my chair behind my neatly arranged desk, touched a petal on one of the roses I had brought for the first day, and wondered if I should have become a teacher. Was the only cure for problems like this to get out? I told myself I'd suffer for one year, and after my marriage that next summer I'd do something more rewarding.

"They got to you, didn't they?" It was my colleague from across the hall. I nodded in reply.

"Look, don't worry. There are only fourteen of them, and most of them won't graduate anyway. Don't waste your time with those kids. Put your energy into the good kids."

"What do you mean?"

"Those kids live in the shacks, in the fields. They're migratory labor, pickers' kids. David, the one on the floor, had pestered Mark's sister while they were picking beans together. I had to tell those guys to shut up at lunch today. Anyhow, they only come to school when they feel like it. Just keep 'em busy and quiet, and everything will be fine. If they cause you trouble, send 'em to me."

Numb, I sat and stared for what seemed like hours, then gathered my things to go home. I couldn't erase the look on Mark's face as he said, "We're the retards." *Retard*. That word clattered in my brain and couldn't find a quiet spot to rest. Its echo was beginning to give me a splitting headache, and I knew I had to do something drastic.

The next afternoon I went to my colleague's classroom and politely asked him not to come into my class again, that I needed to try to handle the kids my own way, by myself. Then I quickly turned away and walked back to my territory, determined to claim what was mine. I left my desk and stood in the middle of the class surrounded by those fourteen special students. I made eye contact with each of them, and then I turned, went to the board, and wrote ECINAJ.

I said, "That's my first name. Can one of you tell me what it is, please?"

They told me my letters were "weird" and that they had never seen that name before. I went to the board again. This time I wrote JANICE. Several of them blurted my name and then gave me a funny look. They couldn't tell what was happening and seemed to fear I was playing a joke on them. They became tense and wary.

"Okay, my name is Janice. I'm learning impaired, something called dyslexic. When I began school I couldn't write my own name correctly. I couldn't spell and numbers swam in my head. I was labeled 'retarded.' That's right—I was a 'retard.' RETARD. I can still hear those awful voices and feel the shame."

"Yeah, so how'd you become a teacher?"

"Because I hate labels and I'm not stupid and I love to learn. That's what this class is going to be about. If you like the label 'retard,' then you don't belong here. Change classes. I don't want you here. There are no retarded people in this room. I'm not going to be easy on you. We're going to work and work and work some more until you catch up. You *will* graduate and I hope some of you will go on to college. That's not a joke or a threat—it's a promise. I don't *ever* want to hear the word *retard* in this room ever again. Do you understand?"

Somehow, after that, I thought they sat up a little straighter.

We did work, and I soon caught glimpses of promise. Mark, especially, seemed to be very bright. I heard him tell a boy in the hall, "This book's real good. We don't read baby books in there." He was holding a copy of *To Kill a Mockingbird*, a book I still love to teach now, twenty-five years later.

Months flew by, and the improvement was wonderful. Finally, Mark said one day, "But people still think we're stupid 'cause we don't talk right." It was the moment I had been waiting for. Now we could begin an intensive study of grammar, because they wanted it. I was sorry to see June approach; they wanted to learn so much.

All my students knew I was getting married and moving out of state. I overheard whispers about presents and flowers. The students in the last-period class were visibly agitated. Most of my special fourteen came from families so poor that the school assistance program was the only guarantee of warm clothing and decent meals for these students. Mark, however, had a plan. On weekends he cleaned the local flower shop, weeded the gardens, and did general maintenance. He had seen the orders for flowers from several of my classes. Poverty is as much a label as "retard," and he was becoming too proud ever to wear an insulting label again.

He called the local funeral parlors and explained that his teacher was leaving and he and his classmates needed flowers for her. He arranged to have several bouquets from the flower car saved after each funeral was over. He also asked for all the "tired" flowers in the florist's shop.

So on my final day of that first year I was greeted by the principal as I entered the school. "Miss Anderson, will you come with me, please. There's a problem with your room." He looked straight ahead as he strode down the hall, and I silently followed.

There was a crowd by my classroom; my Period 7 class was outside too, grinning. Mark said very loudly and proudly, "Miss Anderson, Period 2 got you roses and Period 3 got you a corsage, but we love you more." He motioned to my door. I looked inside the room.

It was amazing. There were funeral sprays in each corner, bouquets on the desks and filing cabinets, and a funeral blanket across my desk.

I started to cry, and they joined me. We all cried. It was one of the most touching moments of my life.

That, however, was not the end. *All* those students did graduate two years later, and six earned scholarships to college. The years have passed quickly, and I'm teaching back in the same area again—this time in an academically strong school not too far from where I began my career. Strangely enough, next year I hope to have Mark's *son* in my sophomore honors English class. Mark married his college sweetheart, and he is a successful businessman. His son has had all the privileges his father never had, and I hope he has the richness of spirit and compassion that his father had in such abundance.

Sometimes now I laugh at myself recalling the end of that first day, that I was thinking desperately of leaving teaching and "doing something rewarding." What greater reward could there ever be than the privilege and responsibility of trying to make a permanent difference in the life of a child.

Janice Anderson Connolly began her teaching career at a high school in southern New Jersey, near Philadelphia. She later returned to New Jersey, where she now teaches at a large high school not far from New York City.

CHAPTER 4

The University School

*

Emma Lewinsohn Frey

I will never forget my eleventh-grade class: Frankie, Ralph, John, Bob, Paul, Coleen, and Diane. The eight of us met in the smallest room of a converted house that served as the school. At the start of each class we battled. They wanted the door closed; I insisted it remain open. They wanted to discuss our social lives; I wanted to discuss literature. They wanted to take me out on dates; I wanted them to develop a love of learning. They wanted to teach me how to swear in Italian; I wanted them to learn correct English. They all teased Diane; I defended her. They tried to make me nervous; I tried to make them learn. It was me and them. Us in the tiny room. I counted the days remaining in the term as often as I counted the unread pages of *The Great Gatsby*.

I knew very little about the University School when I was hired to replace a teacher who had left in mid-year. It was an alternative high school in our state's largest and poorest city. Despite its name, the University School was far from an intellectual mecca, and teaching there was my first experience outside the comfortable walls of middle-class academia.

The students made my first year memorable. Some of them were considered disciplinary problems in the public schools, some were labeled learning disabled, some were alcoholics or drug addicts. From them I learned what it is like to grow up with immigrant parents, divorced parents, alcoholic parents, or no parents. Unlike me or my fellow students in college, they did not take for granted a college education, a nine-to-five office job, a suburban home, or a happy family. They were interested in fast cars, bars, gangs, sex, drugs, and alcohol. They were not interested in *The Great Gatsby*.

I tried to teach the book, clinging doggedly, for technique, to memories of my own educational experience. Every day my students tested my authority and tried my patience. In desperation one day, I changed my tactics and abandoned *The Great Gatsby*. Instead, I ravaged magazines, tearing out pictures of fast, sleek sports cars (Fitzgerald's description of Gatsby's car was the only carryover). I gave each student a picture and asked each one to describe the car and a fantasy journey in that vehicle. They were excited and acted immediately on my instructions. Their pens raced across the paper as they tried to outdo each other in creating a fantastic and incredible story. Language became an instrument for expression of ideas. The students brought to this activity a passion previously reserved for their private lives.

Frantically, I concocted assignments to satisfy and encourage their appetites for creativity and expression. They labored on my assignment while I pushed myself to think of new ideas. They wrote cartoon captions, described pictures from magazines, invented advertisements for their favorite products. Gradually, they began to accept my suggestions for improvement, and we became a team rather than opponents. As the year drew to a close, the intensity of the class peaked as we embarked on writing a complete essay. Diane wrote a heart-wrenching story about a thirteen-year-old girl who committed suicide. It concluded:

Her mother never realized her true fault. She had never realized that talking to her child and listening to the "little problems" that filled her head would have saved her life and restored her will to live.

I cried as I read it. She had expressed so many emotions in the story that I wondered whether it was fiction or near-fact.

I gave these students every word of wisdom I had gleaned in my twenty-two years of living, hoping to inspire them to achieve their goals. They had challenged me in ways I never imagined possible, forcing me to take my own intellectual risks with them. However, despite my attachment to the school and its students, I did not renew my contract for the following year.

The next fall found me teaching at a renowned New England college preparatory school where students nonchalantly drive the fast, sleek cars featured in the magazines I had used as a teaching tool. I remain a struggling teacher, still trying to find new ways to engage my students in a learning experience.

Emma Lewinsohn Frey began teaching at an alternative public high school. She currently teaches at an independent school in Connecticut.

CHAPTER 5

David

*

Nancy Gustafson

"I ain't gonna wash your blackboards for you." The tone was truculent, and the speaker, a sturdy, blue-jeaned youngster, regarded me defiantly from the doorway of the classroom.

"Oh?" Since I'd never before laid eyes on the child and certainly hadn't asked him to wash the boards, a noncommittal reply seemed best.

"I get here early and last year the teacher always got me to wash 'em, but I decided I ain't gonna do it this year." While speaking, he had come to my desk and was examining my markers, uncapping them one by one and putting dots of color on his fingertips.

"Fair enough."

He drifted away to the book table in the corner, selected a book, and leafed through it. Tossing it down, he went over to study a clown poster I'd made to teach the names of colors.

"D'ju draw this?"

"Yes."

"You got paint outside the lines here . . . and here."

In this subtle exchange of personality I did not feel that I was faring well, and I began to understand why the previous teacher had thought board-washing a good idea.

As he wandered back to the book table and began demolishing a display of colorful picture books, I decided it was time for me to ask a question or two.

"What's your name?"

"David Taylor," he replied. "I been in the first grade before, but the teacher didn't like me, so she flunked me."

I remembered the name from my class list. Yes, David was going to be one of mine. The year stretched out ahead of us, ominously.

By the end of the second week of school, David, true to his word, refused to swab any blackboards, but was, it seemed, overwhelmingly eager to offer his services at anything else I could think of. He'd carry things in from my car, water the plants, and—his favorite job— wave the feather duster in furious sweeps over every surface in the room. I came to look forward to these before-school mornings, and I think David did, too. Often he'd boast to me of the things he could do: "I can write all the numbers to a thousand" or "I can drive a tractor all by myself."

It was as if he were "offering" me his achievements in some sort of atonement for the many things he couldn't do, chiefly his inability to read.

Nowadays, when confronted by a student like David, we can call in the psychologist to examine and test and delve into the roots of reading problems. Back then, in rural Kentucky, you just did your best. In David's case, all the methods I'd been taught didn't work, and it soon became apparent that his second year of school was turning out much like the first, with much of the hope and joy in his young life quenched by this inexplicable inability to make any sense of the strange squiggles on paper.

I'd catch him at times staring down at the pages of his *First Primer* with an expression of puzzlement and hurt. This look became more frequent as the year went on and most of his classmates moved on to the *Second Primer*.

I'd learned that David's father had been killed in an accident when David was two years old. The mother had remarried and had three more children. David's stepfather worked at a garage in town and also struggled to raise a yearly cash crop of tobacco on a small "ridge 'n' holler" farm.

At conference time in October, I met David's mother. She was a tall woman, gaunt and pale, with a chubby baby on her hip and a fretful toddler in tow. Her smile, sweet but fleeting, reminded me so of David's. She sat on the edge of a chair and told me she was prepared for a poor report on David's progress. "He ain't never done any good in school," she said. "He's not smart and he just won't try hard." The look in her eyes matched David's, except that in her case the hurt was overlaid with resignation.

A week or so later I mentioned to David that I wanted a kitten. He allowed with great eagerness that they had two litters ready for weaning. I could have my pick. Accordingly, I drove out to David's house the following Saturday. It was a glorious fall day and the rich opulence of field and forest made the shabby farmhouse, derelict barn, and littered yard seem cruelly squalid. As I got out of the car I saw David and his stepfather driving up on a tractor, pulling a sledlike device loaded with rocks. They stopped by the barn. David waved and would have run over to see me, but a curt command from his stepfather set him to work unloading rocks. Some of them were quite large and heavy. The sinews on his skinny arms clenched and he grunted with effort, but he kept on doggedly.

Mrs. Taylor came out of the house to offer coffee. We sat on the edge of the porch in the sunlight, sipping coffee and talking. I asked, and she told me, about growing tobacco. I, a transplanted northerner, knew very little about the process, and Mrs. Taylor often smiled in gentle amusement at my naïve questions. She told of the myriad steps required to get a crop ready to sell at the warehouse—from preparing seed beds in the spring, setting young plants, "suckering," cutting, housing, and stripping. In each of these steps the entire family must be involved and it is all hard work. "David's been settin' and strippin' since he was five," she stated proudly.

David joined us finally, and we selected a kitten with seriousness and deliberation and a great deal of giggling on the part of David's little sisters. As I got in my car, David was called back to work. Driving home, with the kitten asleep beside me, I began to understand a little the rigid limits of the life David was born to—the unceasing demands of work to be done and the relative unimportance of anything else in comparison. They were good people and not insensitive. It was just that the relentless austerity of their lives required a certain renunciation of ease and softness. I felt a sickening certainty that David's eyes too would soon speak of resignation.

In November our school hosted a Grandparents' Day

and I got to meet David's "maw-maw." A tiny woman with fine dark eyes, she had that subtle air of confidence that women who have been beauties in their youth often retain. The way her eyes followed David and the way she touched his shoulder told me she adored the child, son of her dead son. David strutted and showed off outrageously, darting quick glances to be sure she was watching. With a start I realized the "look" was missing—David's eyes were clear and confident.

"He's my only grandchild," she told me at recess. "When his daddy was killed, I tried to get them to come and live with me, but then his ma got married again and . . ." She sighed and added, "David just gets lost in that brood of ther'n and they make that little boy work so hard. . . ."

I recalled her words frequently in the days to come as David, frustrated in his battle with reading, began more and more to divert his energies into misbehavior. At this pastime he proved ingenious, and by the time school let out for Christmas, I felt plainly relieved to have some time away from his mischief, his problems, and his somber eyes.

Near the end of January we got an unplanned vacation—several "snow days" when school buses could not safely travel the hilly roads. That Friday night, as my husband and I drowsed cozily in front of the television, the phone shrilled.

"Did you hear about your little David?" a fellow teacher inquired.

"Hear what?"

"He's been badly hurt. Fell off a tractor. He's been taken to Children's Hospital and they may have to amputate his leg!"

As I hung up the receiver, chagrin gave way to rage

that fate should be so generous with misfortune in David's life.

As it turned out, the doctors saved his leg and he returned to school after only a few weeks, on crutches and with a bulky, grimy cast covering his leg, ankle to hip. His mother brought him in and told me, tearfully, "The doctors say he should be all right now, but it'll never really be right again. He's gonna be a cripple all his life. My husband—he's awful upset. He can't abide cripples." David listened to this passively, eyes downcast, and I was thankful I didn't have to see his expression just then.

As winter slowly receded and sunny days inched us into a gentle and tender spring, David seemed listless and subdued. Although he had grown quite proficient with the crutches, he spent recess leaning against a tree gazing without interest at the surrounding hills. He still came early to school and dusted the room, leaning on one crutch, but he no longer boasted; in fact, he seldom spoke at all.

One morning in late March he arrived late, appearing in the doorway breathless and grinning. "Mrs. G.," he fairly sang out, "I'm goin' to live with my maw-maw! My ma says it's all right and 'he' don't care!"

I guess David's inability to work any longer and his stepfather's aversion to "cripples" had opened a door previously closed. And I could well imagine that tiny lady had been quick to exploit the turn of events!

The move was accomplished that weekend and the days went on, the school year slipping away. In some ways little had changed—reading was still a laborious and frustrating process that kept David hunched over his work with fists clenched and a worried squint. But in most ways everything had changed. He seemed to be able to concentrate more easily on the mysterious paths in the reading maze, because when he had finished there were delights in life—things he could master, things to be praised for, things to laugh about. He had a wagon to build. He had a porch to paint. He had a garden to plant—and not just beans and tomatoes—flowers, too. David himself blossomed.

On a cool, gray May morning when countless raindrops slid softly down the classroom windows, I returned from a trip to the office to find David wringing out the sponge in a bucket of water. "I'm gonna wash the boards for you," he said.

Nancy Gustafson began teaching in northern Kentucky, where she happily continues to teach in a public elementary school.

CHAPTER 6

"The Best You Can Be"

*

Kayla McClurg

I walked down the hallway to the math room and whispered to my colleague, "Um, Dale, can you tell me what stinks in my classroom?" He hesitated only a moment—he had taught enough years to have heard stranger questions—and walked to my room. He returned with twinkling eyes and said, "Do you want it in the kids' words? It's chicken shit. Someone's carried it in on their boots. Probably Leo."

"Leo," I groaned. "I should've known it would be him."

As I returned to my room I wondered to myself how I had gotten stuck with Leo in my first year of teaching. Leo had challenged even experienced teachers, and I was certainly not an experienced teacher. Sixteen years old, Leo was in his third eighth-grade year. That gave him two years of seniority over me, and it showed.

"Leo," I said when I reached the doorway, "put down your desk. Now. On the floor. *Down*." My most authoritative voice and posture. I practiced this voice,

43

this look, every night, and still I remained twenty-one years old, five feet two inches tall, and inexperienced.

In the northeast corner of Iowa, winter comes early, particularly so, it seemed, with Leo in my class. One especially dark day I conferred with his counselor. What was I to do with this boy? The counselor suggested that I give him a task of some importance in the classroom, that doing so would appeal to the kind, helpful person within us all. The next day I asked Leo to hand out the dictionaries. He sauntered to the cabinet and heaved one tome after another across the room. "F—! F—!" he screamed, and *Webster's Collegiate* rained down on unsuspecting students.

The four-letter "f" word had broad possibilities and purposes in Leo's mouth. It expressed anger and dismay, joy and awe. He savored the word and spat it out with as much care as he spat out fat juicy globs of notebook paper; many of them still hung like some intricate art nouveau design from the classroom ceiling.

You might think that a student like this one would lack enthusiasm for school, but he had plenty. When there was a name-the-jack-o'-lantern contest at Halloween, he contributed eight creative possibilities, all of which contained his trademark "f" word. He stayed up late one night making fifty paper airplanes to distribute the next day in the cafeteria. (We were all given the treat of seeing them in flight the next day, laden with remnants of tuna surprise.)

In the frigid cold of a northern winter, school can become a gnawing ache for even the most diligent pupil. But not for Leo. He brought a pig to school and turned it loose to squeal through the hallways. He placed thumbtacks on library chairs and hid behind an encyclopedia, waiting for unsuspecting students to sit down. Leo—and his aftermath—was everywhere.

But one day a strange thing happened: Leo was absent. When I got to his name during roll call, someone said, "Good, he's not here. Maybe he moved away." Another added, "Yeah, I wish he would. Leo is such a pain. No one likes him."

My reaction was one of shock. They had laughed at his antics and encouraged his behavior. *No one liked him?* I'd never thought of this as a possibility. I decided to explore it.

"What do you mean, no one likes Leo?" I asked.

The students began to stack personal accounts of life with Leo on top of their complaints about him, and gradually they pieced together the picture. A picture of a shack on a wooded bank of the Mississippi River. Of a father who drank too much and turned violent with frightening frequency. Of a world of hostility and anger. I began to marvel that Leo was as docile and pleasant as he was.

"It sounds as if he could use some friends," I said quietly. "Where do you suppose he could find some?"

Silence. It was ten seconds before someone said, "I guess you mean us."

"No way!" one of the girls shouted. "He spits too much!"

"But maybe he needs to know he doesn't have to do that to get our attention—maybe we should give him attention anyway," I suggested. "Unless he does something rude—then we'll pretend he's invisible." (I knew this didn't take into account his response when I'd asked him to hand out dictionaries, but everyone deserves another chance.) "How about it? Just an experiment?" A few groans later, twenty-eight heads nodded yes. They'd give it a try. They brainstormed some ideas, and the excitement grew.

The next day, when fourth period arrived, I had to admit I was a little excited myself. In trooped the class, many sneaking glances at me to let me know they had remembered our plan. They would try. Leo, three years their senior, towered over the other students as he made his way through the group. He shoved his way past two boys, tripped a third, and on his way to his seat knocked papers off a girl's desk. They said nothing.

"Hi, everybody," I said. "Let's start today with some questions on the novel. Make groups of four, and you can quiz each other."

Leo stared ahead, looking at no one. Joining or being allowed to join a group is painful for someone who has no friends. Today, though, he looked up in disbelief as all around him he heard, "Hey, Leo, you wanna be in my group?"

"No, he's going to be in our group, aren't you, Leo?"

He looked at me for a decision.

"Wherever you want to go, Leo. It's your choice," I said.

That was the beginning. Everything I had read about empowering students to become teachers of one another was being dramatized before my eyes. These twenty-eight teenagers were teaching this young man how to work cooperatively, how to improve his vocabulary, how to diagram the plot of a novel, how to express himself without spitting. Once in a while he might toss a *Webster's* or swipe someone's pen or elbow his way down the hall, but the class was learning to ignore the negative and praise the positive, and as sure as spring's annual return, new life was sweeping into our classroom.

At the end of the year we had a small awards assembly. Students were honored for perfect attendance, academic achievement, positive attitude, and the like. Students themselves voted on the coveted The Best You Can Be award. Everyone knew who would win. In fact, it was unanimous (Leo voted for himself. I recognized his ballot because there was that "f" word scrawled in the corner of the paper.)

When the awards were presented, the students clapped politely as various classmates won honors, but they gave Leo a standing ovation. Red faced and almost shy, he slowly rose and shuffled to the front. He said nothing, which in itself said a lot.

I sometimes wonder what may have become of him. Maybe he's farming in the quiet rolling hills of Iowa, maybe he's mayor of the town, maybe he's been killed in a bar fight, or maybe he's a standup comic, being paid for using the "f" word. All would have been believable developments in this special eighth grader's life. And I wonder if any of the students who shared in that fourth-period class remember the long dark winter that turned into spring and how they changed the life of a friendless boy named Leo—and the life of an inexperienced teacher.

Kayla McClurg began her teaching career at a junior high school in Iowa. She is now a member of the faculty at Mercy College in New York, and also teaches at an elementary school and at a correctional facility for women in the state of New York.

CHAPTER 7

Adrianna

*

Rosemary Genova DiBattista

Why is it that I remember so clearly the names and faces of the students I had a dozen years ago (my first year of teaching) when I have long since forgotten so many who came after? What is it about that first year that has impressed itself so indelibly on me that I can conjure up eye color, clothing, even smells? Like my own high school years, my first year of teaching has a life of its own. Since then, more than one thousand students have passed through my classroom doors, but Adrianna is one I will always remember.

Adrianna was in my first-period class of so-called average juniors that year. I noticed her immediately, though she sat in the back and tried her best to be unobtrusive. Her beautiful black hair was blowdried in a bad imitation of the Farrah Fawcett style of the seventies. She wore pink-tinted eyeglasses that obscured her large dark eyes. Her skin was olive colored, and she had cheekbones I envied. Unlike most of the rest of the girls, she wore no makeup at all. There was actually a physical space left around her desk, and the boys especially kept their distance. The most I could find out about her was that she had had a poor attendance record for her freshman year and had been out of district her entire sophomore year.

In my class she kept a solid *A* average. By the second marking period, I knew she was an unusually strong student. I had quickly established a rapport with most of my students—I had never been of the "Don't smile until Christmas" philosophy—but by December I still knew no more of Adrianna than what was in her school records. I determined to make her my "project"; my aim was to persuade her to move to a college-track class for her senior year and to consider applying to college.

The first breakthrough in my relationship with Adrianna happened one bitter cold day that winter. I was driving to school in my Volkswagen Karmann Ghia, which had iced-over windows and very little heat. That morning I saw Adrianna walking along, head down against the wind, wearing a pair of oversized purple mittens. Somehow, those big mittens made her look like a child, and I pulled over and beckoned for her to get in. The light changed while we both fumbled to get the door open, and she laughed as horns all around us blared. That was the first time I had ever seen her laugh, or even smile. I was struck again by the delicacy of her face, and I wondered what she thought of herself. I realized she was watching me, too.

Adrianna looked at me sideways and said, "How do you like your contacts?" I had recently changed my look with contact lenses and a permanent. Though students do notice everything, her question still surprised me.

"I'm getting used to them. My eyes get tired sometimes, but I was really tired of glasses, which I'd worn since I was in the third grade."

I was approaching the school lot and feeling disappointed that our time to talk would end. I maneuvered into my spot and turned off the ignition. By now the car had gotten a little warm and for that reason, too, I was reluctant to get out of it. Adrianna leaned over to look at herself in the tiny rearview mirror.

"Since you got yours I've been thinking about getting them." She started to gather her books together. "Now I just have to convince my father. Thanks for the ride, Ms. G. See you in homeroom."

By the following month Adrianna had contact lenses. It was a small thing, but it gave us something in common. Feminist principles aside, I really believed that changing her apperance might be helping Adrianna improve her entire self-image. I wanted her to believe in her strength and intelligence, but first perhaps she had to believe she was attractive. Adrianna herself seemed to be instinctively working in that direction, for one morning she came in looking entirely different. Her hair was magnificent—no more imitation Farrah Fawcett.

"What a great perm!" I said. "Your hair is so soft."

She laughed. "It's not a perm. It's my hair. I just didn't do anything to it." She took her seat, which was now closer to the front of the room and closer to some of the other students.

"Well, don't do anything to it again. Ever," said a pretty blond in the class. She had the kind of looks that are generally valued in high school, but she was now looking enviously at Adrianna. "You know, natural like that, your hair kind of looks like Ms. G.'s." Several of the kids laughingly agreed and Adrianna blushed. I felt pleased that Adrianna was getting some positive attention from other students and seemed to be feeling more comfortable with them. Spring was approaching, and the class would soon be choosing their courses for next year. I suddenly felt a sense of urgency and asked Adrianna to stop in and see me after school that day.

"Am I in trouble?" She looked anxious as she came into the room.

"Trouble? Are you kidding? My straight-A student?" She smiled and relaxed a little. "No, I just wanted to talk to you about your plans for your senior year. Which English were you thinking about taking next year?"

"Senior English, I guess." She frowned a little, and I could see she didn't know what I meant.

"I mean which level of English? This year you're in the middle track, or 'average,' for want of a better word. I'd like you to consider moving up a track to a college-bound class."

"Why?" She looked at me blankly, and I wondered if she was deliberately being dense.

"Adrianna, for a smart kid you're not following me too well. I think you should apply to college. At least think about it. If you take the college-track class you'll do more writing and some research. You'd need those skills in college." I simply kept talking, without stopping long enough to realize she wasn't even looking at me. Her eyes were fixed on my desk top.

"I'm not going to college. I just want to graduate. I just want to get my credits." There was no feeling in her voice, and it seemed that the old Adrianna was sitting in front of me, hiding behind the wrong hair and a pair of big eyeglasses.

"But, Adrianna. . . ." I was about to repeat myself

on the importance of college skills, but she interrupted me.

"I'm sorry, Ms. G. There are just some things you don't understand." In a minute she was gone. And she was right: there was much I didn't understand.

After that conversation I worried that Adrianna would retreat from me, but she seemed even friendlier. Now after class she would stop and talk to me, usually about her schoolwork. On occasion she would shyly ask me a more personal question. One day she asked me about college—what it is like to be at one, what it is like to schedule your own classes. The thought of such freedom seemed both to intrigue and threaten her. I tried to find out more about her home life, but on that subject she was clearly reticent. I gather that her father was a potent force in the household, but that was about all I could learn. I thought perhaps money was the issue, but Adrianna seemed aware she could get financial aid if she needed it. She was going by the guidance office occasionally, picking up flyers and a few applications to local colleges. As a result of my prodding, she did sign up for the college-track senior English. Yet whenever I asked her about her plans, she always gave me the same answer.

"Right now I just want to graduate, okay, Ms. G.?" And that would be the end of the conversation. I couldn't figure it all out. What was stopping her from wanting to go to college?

After a certain point I gave up. Too much of my energy was being directed at Adrianna, and as all teachers know, energy is in short supply that first year. By the end of that first hectic spring, I had all but forgotten my "project." My hopes for Adrianna were consumed by other responsibilities, and before I knew it June had arrived.

During the last week of school, I was alone in the English office when Adrianna popped her head inside the door. I looked up from the exams I was grading.

"Oh, hi, Adrianna. Did you come for your grade?" I motioned for her to come in, but she turned to talk to someone behind her.

"It's okay, sweetie, come on in. You can walk in by yourself." It was only then that I noticed the diaper bag slung over one shoulder, her purse over the other. She led a little boy by the hand. I had no notion of children's ages then, but I now realize he had to have been close to a year and a half old. She sat across from me and the baby settled into her lap.

It took me a while longer than it should have. "So, are you babysitting today?" I said. Adrianna rummaged in the diaper bag and I assumed she hadn't heard me. "Who is he, your nephew or something?"

"He's mine." She said it quietly. At that moment everything became clear—her reluctance to talk about herself, the year spent out of district, the distance between her and the other kids. Suddenly I knew why college was such a difficult decision for her. And as I watched her with her son, I saw yet another Adrianna. It is only now, after having a child of my own, that I understand the look on her face as she held her little boy.

I looked again at the two bags she carried—a diaper bag and a purse. One held a bottle and toys, the other hairspray and chewing gum. Those bags represented both sides of Adrianna, the mother and the high school girl.

She stroked her son's hair. "His name is Frankie."

She went on to tell me about his father and about her circumstances at home. Her own father had threatened to throw her out, but when the baby was born he had fallen in love with his grandson. We talked until Frankie got restless, and Adrianna got up to leave. It seemed that in those few moments she was trying to tell me all the things that had held her back for a year. On her way out the door, she stopped.

"Oh, Ms. G., did you know the county college has a day-care center on campus?" She smiled.

"Does that mean you're going?" I tried hard to sound casual.

"Maybe." She gathered up her two bags and took Frankie by the hand.

"At least think about it," I called to her as she walked out the door.

That night I saw her at the school's graduation ceremony. Before it began, we both stood by the fence and watched the seniors greeting parents and friends out on the field.

"Next year that will be you," I said. Adrianna stood shading her eyes from the last of the evening sun, and that is how I will always see her—tan and slender in a summer dress, her black hair and eyes shining, looking like any seventeen-year-old girl.

"You've come a long way, you know," I said. "You should be proud of yourself." She gave me a quick hug and stepped back.

"I couldn't have done it if it hadn't been for you." Before I could say a word, she left the fence to walk over to a group of friends, only turning once to wave goodnight.

What had I done for her? I didn't know then, but now I think that she looked at me and saw someone she could be. Nothing can mean more to a teacher. Even now, when I get discouraged, I think of her words. After Adrianna graduated, I wrote her a note asking her to stay in touch, but I never heard from her again. I never even found out whether she went to college. I often think of her and of Frankie, who by now must be a fifth or sixth grader. I wonder if Adrianna could ever know what she has done for me, who did so little and got so much in return.

Rosemary Genova DiBattista teaches at a high school in central New Jersey, the setting of her story and her career for the past twelve years.

CHAPTER 8

Answers and Questions

*

Z. Vance Wilson

Around the half-circle of senior English students, every face fell. Only a pencil's nervous scratch kept the silence from being complete and deathly. Someone coughed. I stared at each student's lowered head, waiting for someone to risk a glance.

Finally, a basketball player named Tommy gained the courage. "Did you really mean for us to read it? *All* of it?"

"What do you think I assigned it for—my own health?" The edge in my voice caused it to crack, and it sounded a lot like the voice of a boy during puberty. I wasn't all that much older than Tommy.

Parker laughed. I flung him an eye-to-eye dart and he quickly dropped.

"We thought you might explain it, Mr. Wilson," John said.

"Without any of you reading it?"

"That's what English teachers do, you know," he continued. "Honest. The next day they tell us all these funny little stories about the author and then outline the major themes and point to the important passages and then we study our notes for the paper or the test. They sort of give us the answers and then we do the work."

"Not this English teacher, son."

"Yes, sir."

I turned toward the window, telling myself to breathe deeply. But I couldn't count past two. Even the stunning beauty of an autumn day in Atlanta couldn't soothe my anger or the Georgia pines two or three feet from the window or the mallards lazing on the spangled pond in front of the school or the early color of the hardwood trees singing their way up the hill. No, I was mortally offended. Nature was not joy unbounded.

At first there was a communal gasp. It was perfectly audible, twenty-two senior students sucking air in unison, then absolute silence.

I had stepped back from the window and with a sudden jerk threw the teacher's desk onto the floor.

As I remember the episode, fourteen years later, I am amazed by my audacity as a rookie teacher: the desk wasn't even my own. I was a "floater," a first-year teacher who had to meet his sections in classrooms that happened to be free because the experienced teachers were taking breaks or monitoring study hall. But that thought didn't stop me from letting my anger blow. I grabbed the edge of this foreign desk and tumbled it over so violently that the lap drawer and two of the side drawers spilled their contents out all over the floor. I have a vague, embarrassed memory of two or three compasses, a box of tissues, a grade book, a jar with a dead spider in it, a stapler, and no fewer than five hundred paper clips.

Why bother to look at the students again? I paraded straight for the door and slammed it in their spoiled adolescent faces. Those were my feelings at the ripe age of twenty-four. Then I froze in the center of the hall, suddenly having no idea how to cool my rage or where to hide my foolish new teacher's body, which had abandoned its post in the line of fire.

The English department chair, the principal, and the headmaster all counseled me. I wasn't fired for my infantile rage nor did I quit, but I had to find a way to go back into my classroom and work with my students. They actually began to read—or try to read—their assignments. Chaucer, Shakespeare, Donne, Milton—none was easy even for me, especially because I assumed that when the seniors couldn't answer my questions, I was supposed to.

February was the cruelest month. In the second-floor faculty lounge, the English department chair—we called him Curmudgeon—held court every day, filling the room with cirrus clouds of pipe smoke. In his chair, on the floor, on the table at his elbow, and in his lap lay papers bloodied by his red-ink pen. He was a tall man with gangly arms and legs that stretched halfway across the room.

Without looking up, he spoke as I came in. "How's this cold and dreary month treating you, Geyser?" (He had dubbed me Geyser shortly after the desk episode.)

"Not much better." I fell onto the couch. "And I ought to be in the library grading papers instead of sitting here slinging it with you."

"Of course you should, but you'll sit anyway. It's the human condition," he opined.

"I'll sit, but I refuse to admit it's my human condition."

He paused for a puff, gnawing at the pipe's bit.

"What expectations do you have for your seniors, Geyser?"

I laughed. "Oh, a variation of Chaucer, I guess. 'If gladly would they learn then gladly would I teach.' "

"I take it by your tone you've been disappointed?"

"To say the least," I replied.

"Are your expectations too high?" he puffed.

"I expect them to care enough to try. That's all."

"Noble expectations. But is that what you're teaching them?" he asked.

"I don't understand what you mean."

"Are you teaching them to care enough to try?"

"I want them to see how important literature is to their lives," I said.

"Is that the same thing as teaching them to care enough to try?"

I still didn't quite get what he meant, but I didn't fess up to it then. As the year went on, we had many more informal conversations, during which he made oblique suggestions through clouds of pipe smoke. He visited a few of my classes and said "Good job, Geyser" every time as he left. His only immediate practical advice was to count six seconds after every question I asked. In some ways it seemed rather foolish, but the man was respected as a master teacher and I had a brief but painful memory that on my desk-throwing day I'd been unable to get to "two." The suggestion began to seem better.

Near the end of Joseph Conrad's *Heart of Darkness*,

the infamous ivory trader Kurtz, on his deathbed in the Congo, whispers the phrase "The horror! The horror!" But the truly climactic episode follows Kurtz's death when the narrator, Marlow, visits Kurtz's fiancée in Brussels. Throughout the story, Marlow has said that he despises lies, but when asked by Kurtz's "intended" what his last words were, Marlow lies and says that with his last breath "the great man" spoke her name.

In the spring we had closed the semicircle of our desks to a closer-knit circle with the teacher's desk outside.

"Why does Marlow lie to her?" I asked.

As usual I felt a physical urge to answer my own question quickly, to point them to the passage early in the book where Marlow reminds his listeners that London, the capital of civilization, was once itself a dark and horrific place. I could hear my own sweet voice within my head. "Don't you understand? We build our culture on blindly held illusions."

But instead I did the Curmudgeon count: one thousand one, one thousand two, one thousand three . . . In the middle of my counting I recalled Milton's famous line, the one the *Norton Anthology* uses to illustrate a snail's crawl of poetic rhythm: "Rocks, caves, lakes, fens, bogs, dens, and shades of death." The wait seemed endless.

Just before I gave in to answer my own question, Tommy shifted in his seat. "It wouldn't do any good to tell her the truth," he said.

Oh my God, I thought, he used "good" and "truth" in the same answer. My mind spun. I could allude to Keats's truth and beauty and tell them about his bittersweet love for Fanny Brawne—surely there was a connection there. But then I stopped myself.

"Why not?" I said. And I counted again. "One thousand one, one thousand two, one thousand three, one thousand four. . . ."

"Sometimes it's better to lie about things," John said.

"No, you should always tell the truth." It was Elizabeth, who had invited me to her church three or four times.

"And just because she's a woman doesn't mean she can't face the truth." This time, Millie. "We said the natives of the Congo had a different culture, didn't we? No better, no worse than the European one. She lives in a different culture from Marlow, that's all. It doesn't mean you have to go to the Congo to explore. And the truth of Kurtz's death might have opened her eyes."

"But are you going to tell the truth if it shatters someone else's carefully created illusion?" I said. And then, without thinking, I said, "It might lead to despair."

A terrible mistake. I knew it right away. I had offered an answer, and silence followed. No one knew how to respond to a teacher's statement.

But Parker, the most unlikely candidate, asked his own question: "Do you think we have illusions?"

"No, not really," Mike said.

"This school is built on more than one," offered a previously quiet voice.

"That's for damn sure."

Now I had to say, "Your language, please, John."

"I'm sorry, sir, but it's true—about the school, about society. You're supposed to act a certain way, the civilized way, I guess. Rules and more rules. But lots of them are false. The whole thing is false. Something inside of you, you know. . . ."

"Is that bad?" Elizabeth asked. "I mean, that we're taught to act differently from our instincts."

"Of course it is. We ought to be who we are."

"But then we'd all be savages."

The bell rang. No one moved.

"It's a sham, man. A lie."

"It's the same illusion Marlow gave to that woman, and he said he never wanted to lie."

"He had to lie, he had to." Arthur pounded his desk. "The truth would have killed her."

"But somewhere in the story he says lies smell of death," Millie said.

Suddenly we looked up at one another. I was speechless. And in a second they were gone.

John, hurrying out the door, looked at me. His face beamed. "That wasn't bad, was it, Mr. Wilson?"

"Just great."

"We ought to do that more often. It's nice to see people in this room care about ideas."

I had been under the terribly civilized and common teacher's illusion that I'd been teaching them to care about ideas every day of my rookie year. But for the first time of many in my teaching career, I realized my own lie: two agendas were being conducted in the classroom—mine and theirs. Waiting for the agendas to meet, waiting for them to care enough to try, and waiting for me to care enough to let them try—it couldn't happen while I insisted on answering the questions. It would take as long as parallel lines finding their way to infinity. One thousand one, one thousand two, one thousand three . . .

Z. Vance Wilson began teaching in Atlanta, Georgia, and now teaches at the Madison Area Technical College in Wisconsin. He is the author of a novel, The Quick and the Dead, *and a book on integration in southern schools*, They Took Their Stands.

CHAPTER 9

Learning to Read

*

Patrick McWilliams

From the first day, I thought I knew what my role as teacher was meant to be. I had spent four years of graduate study learning how to tell the difference between good writing and not-so-good. I had learned a great deal about how to revise my own writing. I had learned that a writer has a responsibility to the reader. Now I was to be a professional "reader." My job was to search out the flaws in my students' writing, to notify them of the many errors of their ways, and to enforce my judgment with a solidly objective grade. "You have got exactly what you deserve," says the arid schoolmaster of Terence Ratigan's *The Browning Version* to a schoolboy who wishes to know if he has passed—"nothing less and certainly nothing more." I could have played that schoolmaster.

In the first semester of my teaching, into my hardened hands fell a narrative essay by Laurie. She was the perfect victim for my exercise of critical acumen. Laurie was wholesome, eager, not at all unread, but more acquainted with Nancy Drew than with *Tess of the D'Urbervilles*, and to all appearances ready to accept advice from her teacher. I think I liked best about Laurie her way of puffing out her cheeks when she was wrestling with a tough question in class. I had seen her puff out her cheeks in the same way in sports contests. It was always a sign of effort with her.

Laurie had given me a paper about a particularly satisfying threeday hike she had taken in the New Hampshire mountains. Her essay had not a flaw that care and diligence could prevent: no misspellings, no grammatical errors, no malapropisms. But it wasn't perfect—it was full of clichés.

The great thing, or so I thought in those days, was to find an essay with faults that happened to be within the range of my rather shortsighted vision. In my glossary of Errors My Students Shall Not Commit, the cliché occupied a large section.

The very subject Laurie had chosen was, to my mind, a cliché. In only three months at my first job in New Hampshire, I had already read something like ten narratives about hiking experiences. I made a note to her about choosing fresh topics even before I had finished the first paragraph. The clichés in Laurie's account of her hike were the usual suspects, and like Claude Raines in *Casablanca* I rounded them up dutifully.

"The breeze," she told her reader, "lifted my hair gently from my cheek." And furthermore, "The sunlight filtered through the pines onto the forest path." And, "The air was crisp and invigorating." Also "The climb up the mountainside was tiring but fun, and the view from the top was panoramic."

When Laurie's foot slipped at the edge of an escarpment, she "could feel the adrenaline flowing" as she righted her balance, and "not a split second too soon," she grabbed for an overhanging branch.

I knew my job: to search out error wherever it occurred and cow my student writers into giving me what I wanted. I had searched for clichés—and I had found them. Now I was ready to cow—er, teach—Laurie.

Of course, I didn't know my job at all. My first lesson in that fact came the day after I had returned Laurie's essay. I had given it a half hour of my time, not a bad ratio to her six or seven hours of composition. I had written a long paragraph or two explaining the importance of showing, not telling. I had dutifully explained that clichés are substitutes for genuine narration and description. I had discoursed on the writer's responsibility to give the reader a fresh account of experience. And I had given her a generous dose of green-inked underlinings (not red—even I knew better than that) and a large helping of the word *cliché*, possibly ten times in four pages.

The day after I had returned her paper, with a magnanimous B-minus, Laurie showed up in my classroom just after school. I was surprised. She had not struck me as the type to argue over a grade. I was right, at least, about that. She had not come to argue about the grade.

She stood beside my desk, ignoring my offer of a seat. I felt at a disadvantage. Laurie was a strong, athletic girl. And she was looking down at me now, puffing out her cheeks, with probably the same look she gave a soccer ball she was about to propel with a swift kick.

She kicked. She said to me, "How would you feel if someone asked you to write about something you cared deeply about [I had asked just that when I made the assignment], and then they write 'cliché, cliché, cliché' in the margin after every other sentence?"

I didn't have an answer. Or rather, Laurie knew and I knew that the answer was obvious. But I had never asked myself the question she was asking. I had assumed that my job was to judge and that her job was to be judged (and to be at least respectfully chagrined to know that I knew her every sin of writing). I had so little imagination that I hadn't connected how I feel when my own writing is not well received with how my students might feel. I had lured my young writers into thinking they were writing for a friend; then I had pounced on them like the beadle in *Oliver Twist*. I didn't have an answer for Laurie. I hadn't known my job at all.

After seventeen years of teaching I know better. I know that my job has nothing to do with judging the writing of my students. Like anyone else, I have the perfect right to judge the writing of professionals—the people who charge us money to read what they have written. But my students are not professional writers. My job—my duty—as a teacher is to find the best in what my students have done and to help them see for themselves the difference between their best work and their indifferent work. Students don't need critics; they need teachers. They don't need adversaries; they need readers. They aren't miscreants; they are growing writers. We who teach are not meant to search for faults but for possibilities. It took me a while to learn that.

Patrick McWilliams experienced his first year of teaching at an independent school in New Hampshire. He currently teaches at a public boarding school in Illinois.

CHAPTER 10

Order in the Classroom

*

Andrew Dean Mullen

"To survive around here, you've got to be tough as nails. Show them who's boss right from the start." These words from my supervising teacher stayed with me through my student teaching, but I couldn't seem to put them to use. I sometimes wondered if my fifth-grade students took advantage of the fact that I wasn't a "real teacher" yet and actually sat down together and plotted against me. Just when I'd convinced myself that their crimes must be premeditated, I'd notice that they were very good at spontaneous uprisings, too.

With my student teaching behind me, I started out with a clean slate at a school in another part of town. My former supervisor's words were still with me: I did not intend to face another classroom where I didn't have control.

Day one I read my new charges (fourth grade this time) the longest list of rules and routines they'd ever heard. Yes, we would play games. Yes, we would have activity centers for students whose regular work was complete. Yes, everyone would have a good year, but only if they cooperated with me. I was the teacher. I was running the show. It was the students' job to sit still, listen, and do as they were told. Much to my surprise, they did just that.

After the first day of polite listening, I told myself not to be fooled. Beneath their docile appearance lurked the potential for untold disaster. But days went by without a crisis. Two weeks passed, and still no threatened rebellions. I was in control.

By the end of September the principal, Mr. Williams, was noticing how straight a line we maintained as we walked to the cafeteria. My colleagues praised the class for getting drinks after gym so quietly. Visitors passing by in the hall smiled as they looked in at the straight rows of diligent, orderly students. I was pleased.

It wasn't just the students I controlled. I also had charge of the physical space assigned me. The gray, windowless classroom Mr. Williams had shown me in August was now ablaze with color. Art and science centers beckoned from every corner. Posters lit up the walls. Private reading zones, suitably equipped with pillows, competed with listening centers for students' time and attention.

Best of all, I was fully in command of the curriculum. I filled my plan book with one creative idea after another. Some teachers might make do with commercial worksheets, math drill from the text, and lessons from the basal reader, but I wanted better. Why have students read the science text when I could spend the time conducting some experiments for them? Surely, the skill in the language book could be turned into some kind of game. A few homemade charts might make those concepts in fractions easier to understand.

I might have felt even more successful if I hadn't felt tired all the time. By three o'clock each day the room was a mess and I was a wreck. After an hour of frenzied running around, I'd stop and realize I'd accomplished nothing. I was lucky if I'd rearranged a few piles on my desk. Papers to be graded, charts to be updated, and forms to be sent to the office mushroomed everywhere. Teachers' magazines I'd once devoured eagerly began to gather dust.

Success stories that Mr. Williams trumpeted in faculty meetings—prizes won, grants awarded, commendations received from parents—convinced me I wasn't working hard enough. I gave up Saturdays. Then Sunday afternoons. I stayed in my classroom later and later each day, putting up one more bulletin board, cutting out one more game piece, making just one more set of cards.

The classroom continued to run smoothly, but I was burning out fast. I found myself being resentful of my students, who didn't seem to be living up to their end of the bargain. If I was working so hard, why weren't they? And sometimes I'd look out during my lessons and see unresponsive faces. How dare they just sit there and not fully appreciate everything I was doing for them?

I shared my frustration with Greg, the experienced teacher across the hall. He seemed sympathetic and invited me to observe one of his classes. I didn't want to like his class, and at first I didn't have to. My first impression was of loud voices and of students moving around the room at will. This was a writing class? What was the teacher doing? The talking and the movement didn't seem to ruffle Greg in the least. What was happening here? The longer I stayed, the more I was amazed. Greg wasn't being "tough as nails," and yet this wasn't really chaos at all. Students were writing, critiquing one another's work, collaborating on illustrations, discussing ideas. They didn't seem to need controlling—they were controlling themselves.

"How did you get this to work?" I asked Greg later that day. "If I gave my kids a time like this, half of them would just sit there and do nothing."

"It doesn't always work," he said, "but most kids will cooperate if you give them enough responsibility and enough freedom."

I thought about that long and hard. I thought I had learned that giving a class freedom could only lead to trouble. Responsibility? My students had plenty of that: they were responsible for turning in their homework and for keeping their desks in order. I definitely agreed with Greg about responsibility.

It took me a while to catch on, but the seeds had been planted. The next week I put Amy in charge of straightening books in the classroom library, giving her a stake in running the class. When would she accomplish her task? Well, maybe she could have a little extra free time. Responsibility and freedom seemed to go together.

Matt, my best reader, was always enthralled with the current events articles I cut out of the newspaper for Friday social studies. Why not ask him to bring in some articles himself and share them? Why not extend that invitation to everyone? The novelty of listening to their peers might wake a few of them up.

The bulletin boards that kept me at school so late . . . Mickey and Lanita had asked to help on various occasions, but I had turned them down. I was proud of my room's appearance and was afraid it wouldn't look as nice. But maybe just this once it wouldn't hurt to give them this space in the corner and see what they did with it.

Francis would be glad to use my camera and take pictures for the class scrapbook. Shelley, my gifted writer, would be proud to take care of the weekly report. After all, it was the class's scrapbook, not just the teacher's.

Gloria, who loved to mind everyone else's business, could serve as chief desk inspector, even be allowed to choose her own assistants. Slowly, I realized I wasn't the only person in the world capable of doing all parts of a science demonstration. With a little guidance, everyone could participate.

I was catching on to the fact that what was true for me was true for my students: I worked hard when I felt in control of the situation. And so did they. In a classroom where the teacher did everything, it was only natural that the students stopped working hard. When Andre saw his dinosaurs and ninjas on the classroom walls, his attitude was different. This was now his place, too; he, too, had a stake in running things.

It didn't happen overnight, but the classroom gradually became a happier place for all of us. I wasn't as tired because I wasn't the only one working. My students—most of them, at least—were working much harder. And they were enjoying it.

Four years later I'm still learning. I still want to run the show. It's often more difficult for me to relax, sit back, and watch a student take charge than to bear the entire responsibility myself. This morning I caught myself squirming in my seat when Jessica took two minutes to establish order at the beginning of class. I had to remind myself that the order, the control, when it eventually did come, would be a whole lot easier to live with, easier and happier for all of us.

Andrew Dean Mullen spent his first year of teaching at a public school in Colorado. He currently teaches at an elementary school in Louisville, Kentucky.

CHAPTER 11

Death in the Classroom

*

Judy A. Luster

Death brought the class together. The semester was only three weeks old when I decided the Contemporary World Drama class should read Maurice Maeterlink's play *Interior*. It's a mood play with death as the antagonist and is as visual as any one-act play I know. I'd almost decided to drop *Interior* from our syllabus because of Bitsy, a student in the class. Her twin sister had been killed in an automobile accident a few months earlier, and I wasn't sure it was right to ask her to read a play about a young girl who dies. But I loved the play and I knew Bitsy fairly well, so I decided to go ahead with it, planning to deal with the situation on an individual basis if Bitsy had trouble with it.

The day we were to discuss my favorite play, Jedd greeted me with, "That play sucks. The others we've read are good, but this one . . . I hope there's something redeeming about it that you're going to tell us."

John turned to Jedd, slapped him "five" and said, "You're right! That play stinks!"

Not a promising start, I mused. I turned to the class. "How do the rest of you feel?" There were a few other grumbles, but when I asked if anyone actually liked it, two hands went up immediately. Bitsy responded first: "I loved the play. I even underlined some parts." Alison's hand had also gone up, and she echoed Bitsy's feelings.

I moved to the front of the room and sat on the edge of my desk. The play was close to my heart, and I talked a little bit about why I liked it. I talked about death and dreams and grief, remembering what I'd learned the summer before from Ken Moses, a respected lecturer and grief therapist.

"Grief," I said, repeating what I'd learned from Ken, "is so personal that no one can really understand our sorrow. It is inconsolable. No one knows what dreams died with the divorce or the person or whatever the trauma was. Our dreams are tucked inside our hearts and tied to the future. They need to be acknowledged more than they need to be understood."

I got a little weepy when I talked about grief that was close to me, but the kids took over and began to share their own stories. Before the end of the class I asked Bitsy if she would read us the passages she'd underlined. Without hesitation she agreed and through her own tears read clearly what had moved her.

There weren't many dry eyes left in the room, and Jedd announced he was going to read the play a second time from a new perspective.

A day or two later I gave a test. The students had a choice. They could take a short-answer test that covered four or five one-act plays or they could write an essay. They were to choose one essay question from three choices I gave them. One choice read "Define Death."

Almost the entire class chose this topic. They wrote quietly and with intense concentration for forty-five minutes. That evening, when I read their words, I was moved past the play into their hearts.

Bitsy wrote about her twin's death and the near-nightmare at the hospital. Katie dealt with her sister's drug overdose and the love she felt for her sister, which was stronger than her anger. Julie concentrated on the silver dollar her grandfather gave her on each birthday and how hard he had hugged her the day before he died. Lydia still wept for her boyfriend, who had been killed in an accident a few months earlier. Rob wrote about his younger brothers and that "taking their mother away is like taking their floor or the Earth away." He was running away from the cancer that was killing her and wanted so much for her to know how he hurt. Ken was closely concerned with his own mortality and what the next tests he would take in the hospital would show. Alison held her mother's hand as she died of cancer and had only gratitude for the final months she had been able to share with her.

The room had been full of death. Had I known, I would have been too frightened to assign *Interior*. The next day I returned the tests and asked students to indicate at the top whether I could read them to the class. Most said yes, and that day I struggled to share their worlds in a clear voice that did not get lost in the pain.

They were a gift to one another, and near the end of the semester when Rob's mother died they drew around him with loving support. When I first explained Rob's absence to the class, they set about making him cards and writing him notes. Jedd, still unfamiliar with death, wrote of the "tragedy." Bitsy wrote of his mother dying. Alison drew a picture of a boat with a boy and girl standing in it holding hands. The caption read, "Now we're in the same boat." Rob's journal entry during this time was titled, "The Class Where the People Cried."

I will never again think of censoring a piece from a class because I'm afraid of its effect on one person. Had I known where that class was headed, I would have run in a safer direction, but knowing now where innocence and freedom allowed it to grow, I am grateful I went ahead. It makes me wonder how many doors we've helped to close in the classroom rather than encouraged to open. It makes me remember to take risks. Death enabled this class to soar.

Judy A. Luster began her teaching career at a high school in Connecticut where, twenty-three years later, she continues to teach.

CHAPTER 12

"It Say, I'm Very Mad at You"

*

Anita S. Charles

As I peered out the dull window of the bus on the interstate to New York, I felt the rising thrill of anticipation. I had never in my wildest fantasies imagined that I would be heading toward a teaching job in an inner-city parochial school in Jersey City, New Jersey. Everything argued against it. My preparation had been in secondary education, yet I would be teaching first grade. I was from rural New England. I knew nothing about urban schools. I had never even met a nun. Yet I had said yes when I was offered the job.

Why? I wondered, as I watched the blurred pine trees of the countryside turn slowly into city skyscrapers. Why? I had no answer.

Exhausted, bewildered, excited, I unpacked in the tiny room provided for me at the convent. My window overlooked the small fenced-in playground. On page one of my journal I wrote: December 8 (I had finished my college classes in November); tomorrow I begin teaching.

The next morning I met my students five at a time in order to explain that their old teacher had left and to introduce myself as Ms. Anita. Then I entered the classroom and looked around the room at thirty-three faces, all black and Hispanic. Carla was dancing at the Christmas display board, braids flying. Adrian was crawling underneath the coats he had pulled off the hooks. Pablo was punching Gregory. Lakeisha was shrieking hysterically for her old teacher. Other little bodies were in varying degrees of activity. And I was in charge. I picked up the class roster.

The names! Those of the girls were nearly all unfamiliar to me—Reneesha, Latisha, Lakeisha, Tyeshia, Marisha, Yajayra, Yesenia. Would I ever know who was who?

"Ms. Anita! Could I go to de baf'room?" A girl was at my elbow. Her hair was matted and her blouse was dirty.

"No, sit down. We're going to do reading."

"Sister Barbara said you was a nice teacher! But I don't like you no more!"

I grabbed Pablo's swinging arms and placed his wiry body in a nearby seat. He pounded the desk with his fists.

"Class!" I began, with as much authority as I could muster. "Take out your reading books! *Quietly*, please! Carla, stop dancing now. You, what's your name? Cesar? Cesar, that car is *not* your reading book!" The class became subdued, their eyes expectantly meeting mine. How in the world, I thought, do you teach first graders to read?

"Uh . . ." I looked around the room for the help that wasn't there. "Can anyone tell me what page we're on?"

The weeks flew by me like the trees by the bus window. I frequently was in my classroom until 9:00 P.M., poring over texts as foreign to me as the city culture now enveloping me. I was filled with constant frustration and exhaustion. I found myself faced unmercifully with my own limitations. I yelled often, for I didn't know how else to relieve the stress caused by the incredible energy of the youngsters. Sometimes I wasn't even aware that I had been yelling. However, sometimes there were wonderful moments, when I just stood back and laughed. At those times the energy and noise of the children seemed directed, worthwhile, and even an indication of growth. At other times I could only wonder whether anything at all was happening in my classroom besides a lot of noise and confusion. My only consolation was that there was no time to worry about it.

The Sisters were models of patience and understanding. They taught me to separate the problem children from their behavior. "The child is always good," Sister Barbara would say gently. "The behavior is what we need to work on, and tomorrow is another day."

"Tomorrow" was all too often filled with angry, hurt, hungry, tired, searching children. Above all, these children were, purely and simply, children—precious and curious, confused and amazed, energetic and resilient.

Pablo was the most angry and disruptive child in the class, and with him I worked on daily goals, usually starting from scratch each morning. He acted like a caged animal always on the edge of an uncontrolled outburst. There was no getting through to him; he was too disturbed. But to my surprise I found it possible to feel deeply for Pablo. He was starved, both physically and emotionally, and I tried to remember that I was helping both of us when I showed him affection.

One day a book order had come in with an extra sticker book. Pablo desperately wanted the book, so I struck a deal with him. If he could get through a page of work by the end of the day, the book was his. He had difficulty with even that limited task, but I kept repeating the goal to him. I also kept diverting him from potential problems, sending him on errands and busying him during his periods of tension. The look of sincerity and effort on his face was heartrending. I had never seen such concentration from him. He received the sticker book at day's end, legitimately and proudly, and his usually angry face broke open into a rare and painfully brief triumphant grin.

Carla was another one who began the year with similar problems. She was filled with anger and confusion, and we often said she was "six going on thirty-seven." She had seen too much and felt too much. She had a smart-aleck response to everything, and she frequently paraded around the room, hands on her hips and chin jutting out. At my attempts at discipline, she merely rolled her dark eyes and grinned. Unlike Pablo, however, Carla was *not* hostile and disconnected. She calculated, she challenged, she confronted . . . and she knew exactly what she was doing. She was one of the brightest students I have ever met, and I wondered sadly what would become of her.

In mid-January I gave Carla a pad of paper and told her that every time she felt like saying something that was unacceptable or was inappropriate at the time, she was to write it down or draw a picture of how she was feeling. The approach worked. I began to see a change in Carla. She was learning self-control and self-correction. One day she approached me with the pad and showed me a string of random letters: "It say, I'm very mad at you, Ms. Anita." I nodded solemnly and said, "I see," and Carla spontaneously, in recognition of her own success, hugged me and grinned.

Not all the troubles in these tiny lives were so easily handled. There were cases of abuse, of neglect, of serious learning deficiencies. These contrasted sadly with the bright children, the happy and well-adjusted children in the group. The fact that *all* of them were happy occasionally was a source of strength I drew upon. They had a resilience and a remarkable ability to face adversity and to dream of a good and stable future. It was a hope to build on.

These young children needed help with reading and math, but they also needed much more in their lives. They needed imagination and self-confidence. So we sang, happily and frequently. We recited, clapped, danced, and wiggled. We explored sounds and ideas. We discussed issues and concerns. We drew pictures and made up songs and stories, injecting into the grimness of many of their lives small pockets of joy. I could feel the love growing between us.

The last day arrived, and that evening I wrote my last journal entry of the year:

This morning my kids crammed into the office. All in their dress-up clothes and on their best behavior, they sang "Free to Be You and Me" to the whole school. As they reached the final phrase, several pairs of sparkling eyes glanced at me knowingly. We had all learned a lot in first grade.

Anita S. Charles began her teaching career in northern New Jersey. She currently is an alternative education teacher for the public schools of Portland, Maine.

CHAPTER 13

Sonny

*

Julie Olin Schulz

It was our regular Monday morning all-school assembly in the cafeteria at the elementary school in Southern California where I was beginning my teaching career. I was sitting on the steps by the exit, my usual spot for assemblies. The children had just finished singing "My Country 'Tis of Thee" and were beginning "Take Me Out to the Ball Game" when I felt a tap on my shoulder.

I turned and Orchid was there, smiling at me, with a little boy in tow and a yellow slip of paper in her hand. *Uff da*, I thought, reverting to my Scandinavian background, another student. I already have thirty-three! Where am I going to put this one? In spite of concern with my own problems, I noticed the boy's twinkling eyes and contagious smile. His slightly square face and thick brown eyebrows framed a grin that stretched his whole face into glee when he smiled. I smiled back at him, unable to resist his chubby grin. "Hi, Sonny!" I greeted him, after a quick glance at his

84

admit slip. "We're glad you're here. The other children are in assembly right now. Come in and sit with us." I quickly led him to the first row and told him to sit with the class. The cafeteria seemed dark after the January brightness of the desert sun outside, and I could hardly see the outline of the children's bodies for a moment. I felt rather than saw the shuffle of bodies as Sonny sat on the floor with the rest of my students. During the remainder of the assembly, he joined in the singing and clapping, his face animated.

At the close of the assembly I lined the children up and asked Juan Carlos to walk with Sonny and be his friend for the day. He nodded and pulled Sonny with him to the end of the line. As we walked down the outdoor hallways to the classroom, Carol, the second-grade teacher, caught up with me. She nodded toward the paper I held. "Another one, huh?" I grimaced wryly, nodding. Receiving a new student was a commonplace event in our school. Because of our proximity to the Mexican border and the many jobs picking dates and grapefruit in the Coachella Valley, we had hundreds of migrant workers moving in and out of the towns and schools of our district. Bilingual children constituted 75 percent of our school population. By the end of the school year 45 percent of our students would be new faces to our school.

And here I was, a Minnesota Norwegian whose only Spanish was ¡Hola! ¿Qué tal? ¡Bien, gracias! and assorted swearwords I'd picked up on recess duty. Not only was I unable to talk to most of my students' parents but I had no real understanding of their culture. Home visits provided me with some knowledge of the poverty and fear that existed with these families, and yet I was still quite innocent. My teacher training at a college in Minnesota had presented a picture of a world in direct contrast to the poor Spanish-speaking community living here in California. Still, I was delighted to have my first teaching job. After living in Minnesota for twenty years, I loved the warm January days of the southwestern Sunbelt, and my first taste of independent living.

We walked into the classroom, and the children settled themselves by the calendar for our opening exercises. I turned to Sonny and for the first time really saw him walking. I know the shock my face showed must have hurt his feelings. Sonny limped badly; his jerky motions betrayed a serious physical handicap. I caught the gleam of a metal brace on one leg and saw raised scars on his arms. Before I could say anything, Sonny spoke. "Hi, baby doll! How ya doin'?" he asked cheerily. (I discovered later that after the accident, Sonny's social and verbal responses were often inappropriate and sexually explicit.) Amid the children's snickers I settled Sonny into his seat and watched him painfully manipulate his bad leg around the uncompromising leg of the chair. We worked through the regular morning routine of calendar activities and reading work. I sat near Sonny, helping him find the right page in his reading book and getting him the materials he needed.

As soon as I dismissed the children for recess, I walked to the office to find out what they knew about Sonny. I cornered Orchid, the community aide who had brought Sonny to me. Before she could say anything, the school psychologist came up to us, saying "Julie, I'd like to talk to you about Sonny." I followed her into the conference room. "I'm sorry I didn't talk to you before today," she said. "I'd intended to warn you that Sonny was coming, so you'd be prepared." As we talked, Sonny's history came to life for me in horrifying detail.

Always a bright eager child, Sonny was full of energy that day in March. He was playing ball in the middle of Second Street with his older brothers. The ball was hit across the street, and Sonny scampered to get it. He didn't see the car, nor did the driver see the five-year-old he brutally smashed. The staff at the hospital were afraid he would never walk again, but after four months in the hospital, Sonny accomplished a near-miracle. Learning to walk with a leg brace was only part of it. His cheerful personality was seemingly undiminished. His happy, "Hi, guys!" won him the heart of every adult on his hospital floor. The mature comments he would make were funny to the adults there. Sonny saying "Wanna go to bed, baby?" or "You sure have a nice butt!" was hilarious to them, especially when he followed these remarks with his deep belly laugh that made his stomach bounce.

Sonny was released in July and spent the next five months at home receiving physical therapy and home tutoring. When the medical team assessing him met in December, they decided to place him in a "regular ed" first grade, exactly where he would have been before the accident. So here he was, hopelessly behind the rest of his age mates in first grade. The psychologist advised me to try to integrate Sonny into my classroom as smoothly as possible.

With thirty-three children and no aide, I was swamped with work. Most of my students were barely reading. They had minimal attention spans. Freeing time to work with small reading groups was tricky. As for Sonny, his reading skills were nonexistent. He fit into no group in the room. The tutor had tried to teach

Sonny basic survival reading skills, but the only word he recognized was his name. He remembered some of the alphabet some of the time. And with this, we began.

We struggled. And struggled. And struggled. He floundered in the readiness book my non-English speakers were handling easily. Whenever I could, I had him come to me to drill with flash cards. Color words, number words, *the*, *is*, *an*, *and*. The other students helped him in spare moments. We wrote stories he dictated and tried to get him to read them back. No luck. His journal was a meaningless scribble. The connection between spoken and written vocabulary made no sense to him. He would work with an audiotape, replaying words over and over in odd moments of the day. His progress was so slow that I was beginning to lose confidence in my teaching skills. Try as I would to tell myself that it might be his head injury that was impeding him, I felt like a failure. Hampering the process was my lack of knowledge about how to teach reading. I was confused by the mixture of whole language, phonics instruction, and basal reading programs that were available in our school. Every teacher there used a different system, or so it seemed. I was too embarrassed about my ignorance to ask my colleagues for help. To complicate matters further, I was making Sonny's academic achievements (or the lack thereof) a measure of my achievement as a teacher; I felt humiliated that there was so little change. I wanted to be a truly innovative teacher, one whose students excelled academically and were wholly involved in their learning. My ideals and my skills didn't match up. My dreams of being an extraordinary teacher were evaporating in the reality of Sonny's lack of development.

Surprisingly, Sonny still seemed totally unaware of meager progress. He was well accepted by his peers. Sonny's, "Hi, guys! Wait for me!" was heard all over the playground. No one ridiculed his brace or limp. He was welcomed in all of the T-ball games at recess, and the children cheered when he made it around the bases for a run. And though his remarks continued to be inappropriate, the adults in the school liked him, too. When a rabbit in our room had babies, Sonny almost knocked the principal over in his haste to tell her of the event. "Our bunny is a mama!" he announced with a shining face, "How did you like that, baby!" The principal couldn't help laughing at the boy's excitement. His smiles sparked smiles in adults and children alike as he limped around the school grounds.

In May we began preparing for a big event in the students' lives. The children were practicing reading an entire book out loud. The goal: to read to our kindergarten ' 'little buddies." The children's excitement pleased me, and I watched with joy as they worked with greater concentration than they had all year. They wanted to impress the kindergarteners (the "little kids" as they referred to them from the superior vantage point of being one year older). Sonny, of course, wanted to read to them, too. I found an old Ginn Magic Circle book with no words called *The Bumbershoot*. I told Sonny he could make up a story, which we would type into the book, and he could then have his own book to read. He diligently practiced his story with the others.

Finally, the big day came. Books tucked under their arms, my children skipped to the kindergarten compound. Judy, the kindergarten teacher, and I paired off the children, and my students began to read. I walked around snapping pictures. I watched Sonny animatedly "reading" his book to his little buddy, knowing full well that he had memorized his story and that the printed words had no meaning at all for him. His arms waved excitedly as he got to the part where the rain began to fall and the bumbershoot was opened. As I watched, he finished the book, looked up at me, and grinned. He beckoned me over and whispered in my ear, "Mrs. Schulz, I can read!" I hugged him, feeling great tenderness for my proud little guy. As his kindergarten buddy said, "Read it again, Sonny," I watched him and smiled. He entertained her for twenty minutes with the same story over and over.

Sonny played a central role in my first year of teaching. Although I continued during that year to feel that Sonny's failure to read was an indication of my failure as a reading teacher, I now have forgiven myself for not being able to give Sonny any measurable skills in reading. Central to my forgiveness is the realization that I had encouraged Sonny's belief in his own capabilities. He *thought* he could read. I hadn't destroyed his determination and pride, the qualities that had enabled him to walk again. I hadn't given him a feeling of humiliation about not being able to read nor had I ever stopped trying to teach him to read. I had ignited his interest in reading and given him an appreciation of the magic of stories.

The pride and confidence that gleamed on Sonny's face stays with me as a reminder of the lessons I have learned about boundaries between a teacher's efforts and a student's progress and about pride, both my own and that of my students. If I had one piece of advice for first-year teachers, I'd tell them to give themselves credit for what they do *right* and to remember that inspiring in students an excitement about learning is no small thing.

Julie Olin Schulz began her teaching career in Southern California. She is now in her sixth year of teaching at a public elementary school in Minnesota.

CHAPTER 14

Johnny Carson
Was My Mentor

*

Ronald D. Thorpe, Jr.

Could I teach? Of course I could teach. I had been a student for seventeen years, and for most of that time I had been a good student. This was my reasoning as I began my new job as a teaching fellow in Classics at a well-known boarding school.

The first clue that I was ill prepared for the job came on my first night at the school. I was in my dorm suite, listening to the creaking sounds of the cavernous building that would soon be home to eighty-five boys, eighteen of whom would be my charges, when I suddenly realized I had spent the summer reviewing Latin grammar but had given no thought to my role as a counselor. What would I do if a kid overdosed on drugs? Ran away? Attempted suicide? Came in drunk? Choked on a piece of food? Cracked his head on the floor of the shower stall? Anxiety turned to panic as my thoughts raced through a catalog of horror stories resembling those published in the *National Enquirer*.

I got up and looked over the names on my dorm

roster. The boy across the hall was named Castro. I wondered if he was related to Fidel. One of my two proctors was an eleventh grader named Mike, but I couldn't pronounce his Asian surname. I tried to memorize all the boys' names and their room numbers. The place was empty, lifeless, dark. It smelled of old carpets, pillows, and mattresses. The wavy glass window in the bathroom door looked black. I half expected someone to jump out from behind one of the doors as I walked quickly back to my room.

Daylight made the building look better, made me feel a bit less inadequate. I was arranging some books on my school-issued shelves when I heard a knock, followed by the door opening. A cheerful, round-faced boy came toward me. It was Mike, the proctor. His first question caught me off guard: "What should I call you? Ron? Or what?" I managed to stutter, "Ron." The sound was still on my tongue, and I was already furious with myself. My statement seemed to have been a mistake, but I felt it would be worse to reverse myself and look wishy-washy. I tried to recoup by acting a little aloof, but Mike washed that away with his big smile and contagious laugh.

The next day the dorm filled up with parents and kids and other resident faculty. Being busy kept me distracted from confronting my anxieties. The head of the dorm was a tall, athletic man from North Carolina, with a nice way of creating confidence about him. The other three residents were new to the school but even the one who, like me, was new to teaching appeared more relaxed, better prepared to deal with dorm life than I was. My nervousness was reflected in the inappropriateness of my attire. If I wore a coat and tie to a faculty event, everyone else would be there in shorts. If I went casual, the crowd was formal.

The next day my trepidations about dorm life had a competitor in my new worries about the classroom. When I got my class lists, I was startled to see that my brother Chris, a senior at the school, was in my first-period class. Despite my surprise, I was secretly pleased. He would be good support.

On the Sunday after classes began, I was sitting in my apartment grading my first set of quizzes when I heard some noise coming from the Common Room down the hall. I went to investigate. As I walked through the doorway, I saw two ninth graders rolling on the floor, beating the daylights out of each other. Four or five other students were standing around cheering. With my heart pounding, I broke up the fight and dragged the two down to my room. As I tried to talk with them about their behavior, I noticed that a rich flow of blood was pouring from the nose of one of them. The more important fact is that it was pouring all over the papers I had been grading. I sent the boys off after a short but stern lecture, and their laughter was still in the hallway as I turned my attention to the bloodied quizzes. Most of them simply couldn't be saved, so I tossed the whole bunch into the wastebasket.

My students howled Monday morning when I told them the story of the quiz papers, and I felt surprisingly comfortable talking to them about the incident. They seemed to find the story—and me—witty and entertaining. Their response felt good. This was probably the start of my vision of myself as a stand-up comic, one who dealt with the humor of the ablative absolute, the passive periphrastic, and the hilarity of the subjunctive mood. My colleagues were kind and supportive, but no one ever sat in on one of my classes, and no one suggested that I ought to observe anyone else's classes. So my primary source of feedback was my brother.

Chris gave me lots of comments, usually unsolicited, about how I was doing. Sometimes I was "boring," but mostly he assured me that I had a good way with the class. One day he said, "You know, I can always tell when you've watched Johnny Carson's monologue. You're really 'on' on those days." I took this comment as a compliment; I began to become conscious of my own Carson style and made an effort to take a break at eleven-thirty each night to watch the opening of *The Tonight Show.* Just as watching Bjorn Borg had helped me with my rhythm on the tennis court, I felt Carson was helping me in the classroom.

It was quite some time—several years, I'm sorry to have to say—before I realized I had been doing a fine job entertaining my students but a lousy job teaching them. When I think back on that first year in particular, I cringe at the shallow concept I had about what teaching required, and I still feel guilty about what I didn't give those young women and men in my Latin classes. They learned something, of course. Academically talented students have a natural ability to learn even when the teacher works against them, as I'm now sure that I did. My passion for the Latin language and literature was an important model for them, but otherwise I was an inadequate teacher because I hadn't yet made the connection between learning and teaching.

Memories of my experiences from that first year of teaching loom large now in the way I teach, but they are even more important to me in my role as dean of faculty in my present school. I have used my memories of my early uncertainties in designing a new faculty orientation program. More than anything, I try to help beginning teachers see differences between teaching and entertaining. Talented though Johnny Carson is, he may be a questionable mentor for a novice teacher.

Ronald D. Thorpe, Jr., taught Latin during his first year of teaching, at an independent school in Massachusetts. He is currently an administrator at a school in Connecticut, and he continues to teach.

CHAPTER 15

Plagiarism

*

Ted Fitts

The kid, a high school junior, didn't want to be there any more than I did. In fact, since Steven had caused the whole business, I was a bit surprised to see him, accompanied by his father, heading toward the conference room at school that morning.

"Hello, Mr. Morgan," I said, straining to be pleasant. I wasn't too thrilled to see the father either. I had been working hard all year, was tired, and didn't want to end my first year of teaching on this note of confrontation. And I particularly disliked the "term paper plagiarism" that this conference involved. The whole issue stank like humidity after two weeks of rain. Since we'd just endured similar weather in an unair-conditioned classroom, it was even harder to feel charitable. I hoped I could just tell him that his son had cheated and hadn't worked very hard anyway, and we could get the unpleasantness over with.

"Come on into the dean's office, Steven," I said. The dean had arranged for the conference, promised to attend, and then disappeared to get his car muffler fixed. He didn't want to be there either, and rank has its excuses. His secretary had just whispered of his absence to me as I saw Mr. Morgan striding purposefully down the hall. I made some slight apology for the dean's absence to father and son and watched Steven slink unhappily into a chair in the airless room.

He dropped into the middle one of three uncomfortable chairs all directly in front of the dean's desk. Like the threadbare fabric of his faded blue jeans, Steven was worn and weary. Mr. Morgan murmured with resignation about his son's untucked purple shirt and then gazed at me over the top rim of his own tortoiseshell spectacles. "Now, what is this all about? I understand there are some procedural incongruities in Stevie's term paper on Prohibition."

"Well," I said, hoping slight humor might ease the tension, "what should have been 'prohibited' was the use of an author's words without attribution."

He glared at me. "I'm a lawyer, you know, and I'd like to understand more about the nature and scope of this activity."

"Well, Mr. Morgan," I sighed, "here it is." I knew I'd have to explain it all to him, though Steven had already admitted to me days before that he had copied sentences from a book and had given no credit to his source. The boy slumped farther in his chair, looked anguished, and started to speak, "You know, I didn't mean to do it—I just got confused. . . ."

"Hold on, son," Mr. Morgan said patronizingly. "Let's hear the evidence."

So I read Steven's first paragraph, and then I read the identical paragraph from the opening page of a book on Prohibition. Both discussed "debauchery and degradation." It wasn't even an especially good discussion. I sighed again and said, "He left out the word 'it' once. Otherwise, they're exactly the same."

Mr. Morgan tried to look confused. "Ah, yes. Now just exactly what is plagiarism? I mean, how do you know?"

This is worse than I had anticipated, I thought. I felt stuck and alone. "Oh, I'm sure you know the definition of plagiarism, Mr. Morgan. It's the use of someone else's words or ideas without acknowledgment."

"Well, when I was at college there was never an instance of this sort of thing. Ol' Henry Ford, of course, paid someone to take his exams, but plagiarism never occurred," he said lightly. Then he took the offensive. "Now, I'm sure you must have some academic standards here in this school."

I felt confused by this double-talk but could only plow ahead. "Yes, sir, we do. His adviser, and I his English teacher, discussed plagiarism with Steven—and with all our students—at the beginning of the semester. Anyway, there are two more paragraphs here that Steven apparently copied word for word. Shall I read them?"

"Mr. Fitts, I think something should be clarified here. I don't support my son very often. Not much at all. Now maybe I—"

"Dad!" Steven interrupted in distress. His face was contorted in embarrassment.

I, too, was shocked. Mr. Morgan had precisely identified my major complaint about his treatment of his disorganized, punk-rocker son, and now it was about to be turned into his charge of light legalisms.

" . . . Should, but I can tell you one thing. He's an honest boy. He may have . . ." Mr. Morgan paused

". . . an earring in his left ear, but you can't say he's not an honest boy."

"Mr. Morgan, I like Steven. I just wish he hadn't plagiarized on this paper."

The lawyer-father was silent for a moment. Then he said, "Perhaps you can tell me this. Since my son *seems* honest, though he has told me—and I'll tell you—that he has cheated on various tests . . . but that's different, of course. What I want to know is this: what did Stevie *know* about plagiarism . . . and how long has he known it?"

I felt out of my depth and could think only of how many of the Watergate arguments had sounded to me. I tried to collect my thoughts and remain calm.

"As I told you, Steven knew what he was doing. His teachers had explained plagiarism to him. I myself told all my students the penalty for it was a zero on the paper. Everyone knew this before starting the paper. I'm not sure exactly what you're asking me, Mr. Morgan."

"I see no evidence that you have considered his intent."

"How am I supposed to fathom that?" I replied testily. "I don't think he was trying to escape from *all* his responsibilities, but you've seen the evidence of his copying before you."

Steven broke in, "Yeah, and I've never been caught at anything like this before. Why didn't anyone ever say something before now that this grade counts so much? It's going to just kill my average!"

"Steven, you're a junior in high school," I reminded him. "You've often been told about academic integrity. Trying to shift the blame to someone else merely makes—"

"Mr. Fitts!" the boy suddenly interrupted, with great agitation. He was more animated than I'd ever seen him. "Mr. Fitts, there's a caterpillar crawling up your leg!" He stared intently at my trousers, alert with curiosity, and then returned to his slouched position.

Mr. Morgan glared at his son. Steven shook his head, and his shaggy punk-rock hair covered his eyes. He was right though. As I stared down at my pants, I could see a caterpillar crawling steadily upward. In the fluorescent light of the conference room the caterpillar radiated iridescent blue and brown like cheap jewelry.

"Steven," I smiled, "you're right." I plucked the creature off my knee and tried unsuccessfully to intercept Mr. Morgan's hostile looks at his son. "Good observation." I placed the squirming caterpillar on the top of the dean's desk. Steven sat silently banging his knees together until his father turned back to me and began his assault again.

"Now, I fail to see that you have adequately considered intent," Mr. Morgan continued. "Wouldn't you agree with me that my son had no intent to deceive?"

"Mr. Morgan, did you read about the student at Princeton who recently used the same justification?"

"Yes. And in that case I believe four of eleven pages had been plagiarized, if my memory serves me correctly."

"Oh," I responded, "so you're saying that the degree of plagiarism, not the intention, is the issue?"

"That would be imprecise," he asserted, "but it's true you've found only three faulty paragraphs in ten pages." He paused, seeming to be studying the caterpillar on the desk. It had stopped writhing. "That hardly seems sufficient for a finding of fault." The caterpillar righted itself and began a slow journey across the length of the desk.

"There *are* several other places in which Steven writes down an idea that is not his own," I explained. "But whether we're talking about copying of wording or of an idea, all he had to do was to give credit for those words or thoughts. The class had thoroughly gone over the proper procedure for footnoting."

"Wait one minute," Mr. Morgan said, glancing again at the caterpillar. His tone to me grew sterner. "What do you mean using someone else's ideas? I do that all the time at the office. I see an idea; I take it. There's nothing wrong there. That's certainly not plagiarism!"

"Well," I tried to speak slowly, "in fact it is. If you've seen our student handbook—and I know Steven has— it discusses both 'word' and 'idea' plagiarism. I can't seriously accept that you're suggesting that using someone's original insight about the repeal of Prohibition as your own would not be stealing it." As I methodically continued to explain the school's viewpoint, the caterpillar gradually crawled toward Mr. Morgan. His son's eyes followed it.

Mr. Morgan continued to snatch brief looks at the caterpillar as he addressed me. "Such a standard as 'idea plagiarism' is void due to vagueness." The little animal's travels had it heading directly for Mr. Morgan's corner of the desk. He kept glancing at it with the wariness of a pitcher checking the runner at first base. He became increasingly agitated, and began to ramble as he aggressively flipped Steven's term paper page by page as if it were a legal brief. "You'd have to prosecute everyone who ever wrote a paper," he asserted.

Mr. Morgan seemed pleased with his approach. Now he wasn't even looking at me or at Steven anymore. His arms gesticulated with nervous excitement as the caterpillar drew into range. "Do you know what this is going to do to his grades?" The caterpillar continued dangerously close to the lawyer's right hand. "Did you consider," he said, his big hand casually trying to assassinate the bug, "what this would do to his record?" He missed. Undeterred by the near brush with death, the caterpillar crept across the threshold of vulnerability. Mr. Morgan didn't even preface his next blow with another sentence. Fully focused now, centered on the target, he smacked the caterpillar—hard—with the heel of his hand.

"Dad!" Steven exclaimed. "You're killing the caterpillar!"

Mr. Morgan didn't even hear him. "Have you even considered the effect of this assignment?" He resumed speaking, good for another twenty minutes on points of law and precedents. I remained silent. Steven slumped in his chair, stolid and sullen, staring at the caterpillar, now in the final throes of death.

Ted Fitts teaches and directs college counseling at a school in Providence, Rhode Island, the setting of his first year of teaching fifteen years ago.

CHAPTER 16

The Forest and the Tree

*

Elizabeth L. Esris

Some lessons can't be planned. Issues that can arise in a classroom call upon skills that can be learned only from experience. It is the teacher's databank of human qualities—compassion, love, purpose—that must be tapped into during these times. I learned this early in my first year of teaching.

I was working as an eighth-grade English teacher in a solidly middle-class suburb of Philadelphia. There, perhaps surprisingly, I was compelled to confront a series of thefts and incidents of destruction in my classroom.

Most of the incidents were fairly minor, but they continued over a period of time, and I became increasingly disturbed and disillusioned by the fact that my students would violate my property and that of their classmates. Students were upset, too, for it was their book club money that had been taken from my desk, the hooks for their coats that had been ripped from the wall, and their papers that had been randomly scribbled across before they could even be handed in for grading.

The problem was particularly upsetting to me because I felt that I had a good relationship with my students. I had consistently tried to promote an atmosphere of respect in the classroom, and my students had seemed to respond. They were enthusiastic in my classes, and they seemed to savor individual time with me.

I had attempted to deal with the problem by using class discussion to reinforce the idea that the thefts and destruction were wrong and that I would hold in confidence confessions from the culprits. I assured the class that I wanted to help them, not punish them. Nothing came of my lectures on ethical behavior; indeed, more minor incidents occurred.

One Monday I brought a case of canned soda to the classroom, planning to use it on Friday for an end-of-unit celebration. The closet in which I stored it was reserved for my private use, yet after lunch that day I saw that most of the soda was gone. Once again, I felt angry and upset. How could a student decide that his or her immediate desire warranted theft?

I didn't try to hide my anger as I asked each class if anyone knew who was responsible. Many students in each class expressed genuine disgust, but there was no response to my requests for information.

I couldn't sleep that night, and my anger and sadness let me know I had to do something, but I wasn't sure just what. Talking to the class had been futile, and an earlier involvement of the headmaster had elicited nothing but silence from the students. Working my way through hurt and anger, I decided to abandon the role of classroom teacher and try, as a human being, to reach each student on an eye-to-eye, one-to-one basis.

The next day I began class by asking students to

move their desks in a way that made each of them completely isolated from the others. Then I told them that the entire period was to be held in complete silence. I put a paper on all the students' desks. At my signal they turned it over and looked at it as I read it aloud. Next, I told them to begin writing without any questions or talking. The paper read as follows:

Throughout this year quite a few instances of property destruction and theft have taken place in this room. Book club money has been taken from my desk, hangers have been broken, coat hooks have been ripped from the walls, the room has been spattered with Wite-Out, and soda has been stolen from my closet. These are not humorous acts of mischievous fun. This is theft and vandalism.

I am asking you to respond to these acts by either admitting your involvement in them or by discussing your feelings about them. Expression of concern or guilt on this paper will result in a conference between you and me to discuss issues of right and wrong. Please look into your heart, the part of you that really defines who you are, and take a step that may change your life for the better.

The silence during the classes that day was overwhelming, and the intensity of the students was remarkable. During class breaks I sensed a seriousness I had never before seen in my students, and more than one came to me to thank me for giving them the chance to speak their hearts in private.

The papers were extraordinary. I can't be certain,

but I think every "criminal" took off his or her mask and seemed relieved at the chance to do so.

If nobody found out, I would tell someone real soon. . . . Why did I do it? . . . I took the money from your desk. I was going to return it the next day but I couldn't bring myself to do it. Please, I want to talk to you.

Another student:

I was involved with the [Wite-Out] incident the other week. . . . I also broke some coat hooks. I want to be honest with you like I have been the whole year. I have slipped a bit in my judgments of right and wrong. . . . I'm sorry for what I've done and I hope all of this is soon straightened out for good.

In addition, students not involved were grateful for the chance to write about their own outrage and hurt.

I'm glad you are being so serious about this because it seems as though kids can get away with a lot in this school. It's about time someone decided to let people know what they're doing and how wrong it is.

Another student:

What can I say? Stealing is wrong, and I believe those who steal have small hearts and no dreams. I hope the parties involved are punished, but I also feel pity for those who steal.

This encounter was extremely productive and moving. While not revealing the content of individual papers, I told the headmaster the results. He agreed that something positive was occurring and granted my request that he arrange coverage for me the next day so that I could hold individual conferences with all the students.

During the conferences I looked each of the students in the eye and discussed what he or she had written. I urged those who had admitted to wrongdoing to think hard about what they had done. I encouraged them to nurture what was finest in their characters and to talk to parents, teachers, and advisers when they felt unsure of problems and issues. Those students who had not been involved were asked to continue to exercise good judgment and to keep open lines of communication with adults whose standards they valued.

We opened our hearts to one another and spoke our feelings about right and wrong. Some students shed tears, and I felt my own eyes fill as well.

Elizabeth L. Esris began her teaching career eight years ago at a school near Philadelphia, Pennsylvania, where she still teaches.

CHAPTER 17

The Ultimate Challenge

✳

Polly Rimer Duke

"Polly, you've got to learn how to say no. You'll get pneumonia if you keep this up, and then you won't be helping anyone!"

There was certain wisdom in my husband's words, but how could I refuse the imploring looks of twenty-two adolescent girls. Here they were, at boarding school, miles from their nearest relative, lost in a chaotic whirlwind of peer pressure, college pressure, parental pressure, and hormones. They needed the reassuring touch of a gentle, generous, levelheaded teacher and housecounselor. I was to replace their mother, become their friend, counsel wisely, and bake dozens of Toll-House cookies. Simple.

Unlike most years, that fall—my first year of teaching—I had gotten bronchitis only once. In fact, I was feeling pretty good about myself. French grammar was gradually coming back to me, I knew the names of at least half the buildings on campus, and I could even decipher the cafeteria food: ketchup meant beef, mint jelly meant lamb, tartar sauce meant fish. Now it was December. The term would soon draw to a close, and I was eagerly awaiting Christmas vacation and a chance to sleep, see my family, and read something other than high school French texts.

As often happens in boarding schools, that night there was a knock at our apartment door, but it came later than usual.

"I'm sure it's one of the girls. I'll be back in a minute," I whispered to my husband who was waiting at the head of the stairs. But as I opened the downstairs door of our apartment, I could hear the sobbing of one of my students. My nightly duty was not quite over yet.

In her pronounced southern accent, MaryKate exclaimed: "Paaally, I gotta tell ya 'bout Jimmy. . . .He's decided he likes Annie, of all people!"

"Oh MaryKate, that's too bad, but I'll bet there are other—several other boys you might like even more."

I knew there was a hidden motive to MaryKate's arrival. Her boyfriend troubles were a passing concern. Before long we'd be discussing Virginia ham and black-eyed peas, the Blue Devils and downtown Durham. Her pride was too great to admit homesickness, but her body language told the truth. She'd grin heartwarmingly when describing her recent Thanksgiving at home. But when talk returned to pre-cal or History 30 or Chemistry 25, her lips were tightly pursed, her brow furrowed.

When the grandfather clock struck midnight, I attempted to see MaryKate off to bed, succeeding only by mentioning that exam week was upon us and grades soon due. As I walked her to her dormitory room, I hoped not to encounter yet another pair of uncertain eyes, another furrowed brow or demanding expression. These I successfully avoided, but ran instead into a loitering admirer stealthily leaving his girlfriend two hours after curfew.

"I'm afraid the dean's not going to like this one, Jonathan," I warned as our eyes met. "Do you know what time it is? You might have chosen a night other than exam week!"

This was the last thing I needed. By the time I had called Jonathan's housecounselor and given my eyewitness account, it was nearly two in the morning. My contact lenses were stinging, and I was slurring my words. I knew I had an 8:00 A.M. French exam to proctor, and as I slid into bed beside my already snoring husband, I begrudgingly set the alarm for seven.

It was not the familiar buzzer but a ringing telephone that woke me.

"*Allo*, Polly," said my department head as politely as possible. "*Tu sais qu'il y a un examen de français?*"

"*Oui*," I stammered, suddenly straightening into attention. I glanced at the alarm clock that now blinked 8:14. "*Oh, Mon Dieu. J'arrive tout de suite!*"

Never had I leaped out of bed so quickly. I threw on the nearest garment and passed up the hairbrush, the toothbrush, the shower, and all other early morning niceties. As I stumbled into our Subaru, I was already berating myself. The one time all term I had to be late was the morning of my French exam. I prepared myself for the grumbling of students and my department head.

But as I entered the basketball stadium, where the exams were being held, and started down the aisle of intermediate French students, all I noticed were smiles, verging on chuckles. Strange, I thought, that these students, awaiting a rather difficult exam, seemed so relaxed. With each step, the muffled chuckles turned into a decided guffaw. Only after I had distributed the bulk of exams did a colleague whisper into my ear:

"Polly, tu es toujours en pyjama."

Mortified, I looked down to see that indeed the red stripes of my husband Ben's pajamas graced my skinny legs. The fly was open, providing ample opportunity for onlookers to view my upper thigh. (I silently gave thanks for my husband's considerable height, which provided this relatively unoffensive view.) But how was I to sit out the next hour and a half, responding to students' questions and conversing with colleagues in such attire? I decided to borrow the knee-length down parka of a very tall French teacher and pass the time in the back of the gym, sweating, hoping no one would notice.

It was months before I could laugh at my debut as a proctor. Constant lack of sleep made experiences in retrospect take on a Felliniesque twist. Comedy and tragedy seemed to mix as I recalled moments of ridicule and moments of pain. The humor of my ludicrous appearance was now matched in my mind with the challenges I faced every night.

My husband and I had inherited a dorm run for five years by an Afro-American couple. By their warmth and popularity, the couple had drawn many minority students to the dorm. These girls expected to see their surrogate parents' smiling faces when they returned to school that fall. But their beloved housecounselors had decided to relocate, and the kids were greeted instead by a pair of white strangers.

So, Ben and I began the year with two strikes against us. To compound the problem, four of the new tenth graders were white southerners from affluent families whose only previous contact with people of color had been with their family's maid or cleaning woman. By the end of Orientation Week, I was distressed to see factions developing along racial lines. Twice I found swastikas on the sign-in sheet. I knew from a racism training workshop that this symbol was not limited to anti-Semitism but a mark of general bigotry. By early December tension had peaked, and I called a dorm meeting to mediate the crisis.

As we met in my living room, I was overcome with a powerful sense of injustice. I felt compelled to make an analogy between the swastikas on our sign-in sheet and the Confederate flag hanging in several rooms on campus. How could we parade symbols of oppression and racism and pretend we were liberal humanistic thinkers?

To put it mildly, my points were not well taken by everyone in the room. Perhaps because I play tennis and speak French and wear the same style of clothes they do, some of the girls had expected me to share their perceptions or their mindset. They had protected themselves with the comforting thought that they need not extend beyond the limitations their families or previous social codes had provided.

One girl said: "But, Polly, I don't see why the Confederate flag is so bad. I mean, the Civil War was over long ago, and black people shouldn't feel threatened by the flag. It's just an expression of southern pride."

I felt like retorting: "Are you really proud of the Confederate legacy?" But fortunately, Wanda, one of the students of color, responded: "You know, Claire, this flag might make you feel just fine. In fact, you might have no feelings of regret when you wake up in the morning with it hanging over your head. But let me tell you, your flag makes me feel oppressed. It makes me feel like a nobody. It makes me feel like a second-class citizen. Now aren't my feelings real? Or are they second-class, too? How can you continue to do something that hurts others, that oppresses others, maybe not directly, maybe not verbally, but quietly, insidiously, dangerously, and just as painfully as three hundred years ago when my people first started working for your ancestors, when they first started sweating for them, breeding for them, and dying for them right under their noses. I think you owe us a little more consideration. I think you owe us an apology."

Two and a half hours later, after painful words and wrenching personal anecdotes had filled the living room, we were all so exhausted and emotionally drained that our skin colors no longer seemed so important; we had begun to perceive ourselves as equals, stripped to the core of our common humanity. Something had broken that night, and when the girls got up to go, they were closer—a little awkward, a little insecure, but emotionally connected and somewhat relieved. From that night on, friendships began to form between students of different races, and while some girls barely ventured outside their established cliques, never again was there the same tension and anger.

I wish I could say that this was the last bout with prejudice in our dormitory. With a new year came a new group and new challenges. But the lessons from my first year stood me in good stead. The following year I arrived half an hour early to every exam. I now spend three hours in September with all the members of the dorm, laying ground rules of appropriate and inappropriate behavior. If the students learn anything during their years here, I hope it will be to live and pursue their goals in harmony with others, not in separation. If I have learned anything over the past three years, it's this: laugh a lot at yourself, admit your many weaknesses, but hold on to your convictions, and be sure to check your lower garment before leaving the house.

Polly Rimer Duke began her teaching career five years ago at an independent school in Massachusetts. She is currently a graduate student in education at a major university in New York.

CHAPTER 18

"Welcome to the Sixth Grade"

*

Brad Wilcox

"Men get all the breaks!" the veteran teacher announced to me. A cold greeting. Her stare stabbed like an icicle.

"Hello," I countered, extending my hand. "I guess we'll be teaching together this year."

"I swear, all you have to do is wear pants and walk into an elementary school and they hire you! It makes me sick!" I would have responded, but she turned her back to me and stomped off down the hall. I exhaled and pocketed my outstretched hand. "Welcome, Mr. Wilcox," I said to myself. "Welcome to the wonderful world of professional education."

Who would have imagined that the biggest challenge I would face during my first year on the job would not be students, but fellow teachers? Fresh from the university, I had heard horror stories about how hard it is to motivate and discipline eleven- and twelve-year-olds. But I had been well trained. I felt confident in my ability to handle children. I knew the latest techniques. I wasn't afraid of any problems that students might cause. Teachers were a different matter.

"You can't put that there!" Another teacher burst into my classroom. "You can't put the teacher's desk at the back of the room!"

"Pardon?"

"If you put your desk way back there, you won't be able to see them cheating!"

"I don't plan to be sitting at my desk a whole lot," I explained as politely as I could.

"Well," she huffed, "you'll soon learn how things are in the real world," and, like the witch in *The Wizard of Oz* who appears to torment Dorothy and then pedals furiously away on her bicycle, she was off. Her visit did little to calm my Scarecrow brain, warm my Tinman heart, or build my Lion courage.

Next I was told I must not arrange student desks into abutting clusters because "the students might talk too much." I must not use yellow backing paper on my bulletin boards because "it'll make the students restless." I must not put real plants in my room because "they make a mess." I must not put anything into the filing cabinet in my room because "the teacher who had this room last year promised to trade it with the third-grade teacher because she needs those extrawide drawers."

At the opening faculty meeting, I was presented to the group. "Mr. Wilcox will be taking Miss Jackson's place," the principal announced. I smiled my best new-teacher smile.

"You're kidding," said one of the faculty. "She's not coming back? How are we going to do the Christmas program without her?"

After the meeting I waited around to greet my colleagues. Only one came up and spoke. On the heels of the last few days, I lapped up her friendly attention like a lonely puppy. "So . . . ," she concluded, "can I count on you to join the teacher association and pay your dues?"

Where were the kindly mentors who had opened hearts and files for me at other schools during my student teaching? I'd had classes in everything from making bulletin boards to dealing with the severely handicapped. But how to handle professional peers when they were not acting professional?

At home my wife kept assuring me, "You're there for the kids. When you meet your students, things will be different." And she was right. One day the bell rang and there were thirty-five wonderful sixth graders sitting at their desks (still arranged in clusters) and it *was* different. I was happy.

"Welcome to sixth grade." I began the year as I'd rehearsed for months. "My name is Mr. Wilcox." This is what I had wanted to be doing since I myself was a sixth grader. This is what I had trained for through those long university years. "You'll notice," I continued, "my desk is at the back of the room." They chuckled. "I don't want that desk between us. I want to be involved in your learning and involved in your lives."

In the days that followed, I ate with my students at lunch ("Wilcox shouldn't do that!"); I played with my students at recess ("That's unheard of!"); I read with my students in the library ("He's wasting time!"); I even stayed after school with some boys who got in trouble with the principal ("He's undermining the school's entire discipline program!").

My students flourished and I was certain that they were doing innovative things never before done in the history of education.

After one especially successful art lesson, I asked permission to display the work in the hall outside the lunch room. With every tape loop I placed on the back of thirty-five minimasterpieces, I guessed what my self-appointed critics might say: "Who does he think he is? He's trying to hog the best wall space before parent-teacher conferences."

As surely as I predicted the downpour, the next day their reactions came in torrents. Sopping wet, I went home to my wife. "Don't worry," she said. "They're just threatened by you because you're new *and* you're good. New teachers are supposed to be having lots of problems. Let the other teachers know you're not a threat. Just keep being nice to them."

Obediently, I pulled out the Golden Rule, dusted it off, and vowed to start again. As I did with the children, I started looking for specific, positive things I could build upon and reinforce sincerely in my colleagues: "Nice job on the announcements this morning!" "Wow! I like that worksheet you made up." "Man, your kids walked down the hall so quietly." "I heard your class singing great songs. You do a super job with music!"

"I like your bulletin board," I said to Mrs. Icicle Eyes.

"Really?" she asked. "It's just the same old thing I put up every year." She reached out and straightened a sagging border. Then, not unlike one of my students, she added, "Do you really like it?"

"Yes," I answered firmly. As sure as sun beams, the Golden Rule was shining, and things were finally warming up.

That very afternoon, a few parents went to the principal's office asking if their sixth graders could be moved into my class. Of course the students were not transferred, but when the grapevine circulated the request, up went the old barbed wire fence, complete with machine guns.

The principal called me into his office. "I appreciate your enthusiasm. But do you have to be quite so . . ." he fished for the right word, "so energetic?"

"I'm sorry. I don't mean to be a problem. What am I doing wrong?"

He pawed awkwardly through his mental thesaurus. "You're not doing anything wrong. But can't you just tone it down and keep the peace?"

His advice rankled all evening long. Tone it down. Tone it down? Do I have to do less than my best job to keep peace with colleagues in today's educational system? There must be another way. That night I floundered like a goldfish in an empty bowl. Finally, early in the morning, I decided what to do. As a first-year teacher, I was painfully aware of all I had to learn. But I had a few things to teach, too, and not all of them to sixth graders.

I continued to do the best job I could. I worked. I taught. I cared. I waited for a breakthrough moment.

Months passed. It was lunch recess. "Where's Mrs. So-and-So?" I asked the secretary. I was, in fact, searching for Mrs. Icicle Eyes. I needed to consult with her. The secretary shrugged as she continued talking on the phone. I asked the principal. "Check the faculty room," he offered. She wasn't there. Finally, in exasperation, I asked a boy walking down the hall. "Have you seen Mrs. So-and-So?"

Grinning, he came toward me as if sharing a secret. "She's outside shooting baskets with the girls!"

"She's playing basketball with the girls?" I asked incredulously. (Mrs. Icicle Eyes is out there slam-dunking!)

"Yeah," he nodded. I smiled. I didn't say another word. But my smile inside was even bigger than the one on my face.

Brad Wilcox began his teaching career at an elementary school in Utah. He is now a member of the faculty at Brigham Young University, where he teaches undergraduate courses in elementary education and supervises student teachers.

CHAPTER 19

"You Can't"

*

David Gould

"You can't. . . ."

Ask any high school student. These two words are used more by teachers than any others.

"You can't eat in here."

"You can't expect to fail and still play basketball."

"You can't just share your bodily functions anytime you want to." (Yes, I actually heard myself say that once.)

First-year teachers, however, may hear "You can't" as often as they say it. The summer before I began my initial year of teaching English at my alma mater, a high school in New Jersey, I heard countless "You can'ts," cleverly disguised as "advice."

"You can't take any crap."

"You can't start out nice and then become strict."

Much of this sage counsel came not from veteran educators but from veteran bar patrons at the Little Brown Jug restaurant where I had a summer job. Because I would be teaching at a school with a largely

Hispanic population, some of the more bigoted bar clientele felt it their duty to tell me, "You can't teach there unless you know conversational Spanish."

Of all the "You can'ts" I encountered, two stood out in my mind, perhaps more because of the sources than the ideas. My grandmother, a first-grade teacher for twenty-two years, frequently said, "You can't be their friend *and* their teacher." After my grandmother died, my mother took on the responsibility of reminding me of these words.

The other piece of advice came from Frank McNabb, my own former teacher and current department chairman. On the first day of school he told me, "You can't take anything personally." Great. Now I had two commandments I would never be able to follow. I spent the majority of my life trying to be everyone's friend. The second dictum would be even harder—I take everything personally. The first time a student would say that Shakespeare was corny, I would be personally traumatized.

I spent most of my first year bumping—sometimes crashing—into these two maxims. I had one experience, however, that forced me to make my own rules.

My seventh-period English II class was a truly interesting group. They were twenty-four bright, extremely talkative, extremely opinionated sophomores. I saw a problem arising early on with the "no friends" rule. Several members of the class belonged to a school group called Peer Leadership, which met every Thursday night. It was designed to give students an opportunity to discuss concerns ranging from family problems to bad quiz grades to drug abuse. A few of my seventh-period students asked me to come to a meeting, and I quickly became one of the regular adult facilitators. I was immediately impressed with many of the peer leaders, how mature and sensitive they seemed, and how willing they were to help other students.

I found Peer Leadership in conflict with my two main "You can'ts." The nature of the group demanded that I put away my "teacher mask" and become an equal . . . a friend. I also learned very quickly that no one could come to Peer Leadership without taking it very personally.

I became close to one member of the group, a fifteen-year-old girl named Marita, who was also in my seventh-grade class. Just as I had my teacher and my friend personas, she, too, wore more than one mask. In class each day, Marita was a five-foot-tall loudspeaker. Whatever idea popped into her head would immediately be yelled for all to consider, sometimes in English, sometimes in Spanish, but always at maximum volume. At least once a day I would see her small hand flailing the air as she screamed, "Meester! Meester!"

When Marita wasn't calling out an answer, she would be yelling across the room to her best friend Ramona. They would try to squeeze in some major gossip while I tried to teach. Despite assertions that it's difficult to motivate students to write, Marita and Ramona would find a way to pen seven-page notes to each other before I had taken attendance.

Marita's most amazing trait was her laugh. If something struck her as especially funny (and many things did), she would turn red, shake, but make no sound. It was a frightening sight for the uninitiated. The first time I witnessed "the Marita laugh," I thought of summoning the school nurse.

The Marita I saw at Peer Leadership was very different. Whereas I wore my teacher mask in the classroom and my friend face at meetings, Marita was much the opposite. She was all chatter and giggle in the classroom but all business on Thursday night. The dynamo I was always telling to please sit down was a whole new, equally amazing person at Peer Leadership. She counseled students, offered help, and held them when they needed to be held. She calmly and confidently expressed her own fears, concerns, and hopes, and she encouraged others to do the same. The loudspeaker was transformed into a listener.

Marita's capacity for helping was tested one spring afternoon. Something seemed to be bothering her, but the change in Ramona's behavior was more troubling. For the third day in a row Ramona had come into class and put her head down on her desk. At one point she appeared to be silently weeping. Marita made several attempts to communicate with her from across the room, but her friend would not respond. That Friday afternoon I learned the reason for her behavior.

Marita approached me after class and asked to speak with me. Her little frame, so often shaking with laughter, was now trembling from another cause. She said she had to show me something, but she was afraid to. She kept repeating, "She is going to be so mad at me. She'll hate me." After arguing with herself for a few more minutes, she handed me a note written in Ramona's neat, intricate handwriting. I had seen this handwriting many times before in Ramona's essays about her most valued possession and journal entries about Marita or her boyfriend. Now that script was saying things like "Remember all the good times when I'm gone" and "I'm sorry for hurting you."

As she began to cry, Marita said, "I'm afraid she's

really going to do something terrible. I've never seen her like this before."

Trying to appear calm, I said, "We have to do something about this. We have to tell someone."

Marita began crying even more. "She'll hate me for telling."

Teaching, more than any other profession I can imagine, offers numerous possibilities for redemption. A teacher can have a terrific day and a horrible day within the same day, sometimes within the same forty-two-minute period. The lesson that failed miserably in the first period can work beautifully an hour later. The student you loathe one day can say something thoughtful and memorable the next.

Sometimes, small bits of personal redemption are also possible. As I spoke with Marita, my mind shot back seven years. One of my closest friends had committed suicide. There had been no notes offering a chance for intervention, just as there had been no Peer Leadership groups to discuss one's problems. I remembered the feeling of helplessness I had felt. There was no way I would allow myself to feel that way again; there was no way I would allow Marita to feel that way.

"You know what we have to do, don't you?" I asked her.

She said quietly, "Yes, I know."

Marita and I brought the note to the school's student assistance counselor, who was also the leader of the Peer Leadership group. Before long, Ramona's guidance counselor and the vice principal were involved. Within the next two hours, the troubled girl and her parents would be on their way for counseling.

I drove Marita to her job at the local day-care center. She was still trembling. She told me she brought Ramona's note to me because she considered me a friend as well as her teacher. I was happy to hear my grandmother's caution refuted. I drove back to the school. As I entered the building, Ramona and her parents, their arms around one another, walked past me. When they reached the front door, Ramona called softly back to me, "Thank you."

That was the year I discovered that for all its "You can'ts," teaching has an amazing number of "You cans."

David Gould teaches at a high school in New Jersey where he began teaching five years ago.

CHAPTER 20

On Teaching:
A Letter to Luke

✳

Albert S. Thompson

While cleaning up some old files recently, I came across a copy of a letter I had written in 1935. The first few sentences aroused some nostalgic memories, and so I paused to read through the letter before throwing it away. I decided it was worth keeping as a reminder of what a young teacher in the 1930s had on his mind. At the time I was a high school social studies teacher, one who had been teaching for approximately three and a half years. The letter was addressed to a boyhood friend who had just been appointed to his first teaching position. Concerned over getting a good start, he had written to me, an "experienced" teacher, for sage advice and comments on the problems of teaching. This letter was my answer:

January 25, 1935
Dear Luke,

Your inquiry concerning methods of attacking the first few problems of teaching brings to mind an idea I sometimes have wished I had used. That idea is to keep a diary in which to jot down various incidents and thoughts relating to pedagogy as they arise in one's day-to-day classroom experiences. Education courses are often full of high-sounding phrases but give the neophyte very little real practical advice. A journal such as I hint at would be invaluable, it seems to me, and would furnish a suggestive guide to the beginner. And how interesting it would be for the author to read years later, when he had lost some of his youthful enthusiasm and freshness of outlook.

All this furnishes an explanation for what this letter is likely to become—an extended dissertation, a belated attempt to write down not only for you but also for myself some of the things I've learned in my brief experience.

Just where to begin is a problem, so I will first give my reactions to your questions. You wondered whether it wouldn't be best to set up your own system, first giving the pupils a pep talk outlining the methods you intend to use. You are partly right in that. No two teachers do or can use the same methods, but since you are starting in the middle of a school year you must be careful not to make too abrupt a change. All learning, and especially seventh- and eighth-grade arithmetic, is largely the training and development of correct habits, and for you to disregard the habits the preceding teacher has presumably already set up would be wasteful. If I were you, I would find out as much as possible about the methods used previously and continue them at first; you can privately note those aspects wherein you disagree and gradually change your procedure to conform more closely with your own ideas. In that way, you will get the most out of your pupils.

I give that advice because I have in mind alleviating what is probably the most disheartening and discouraging phase of teaching—the fact that results are so intangible and unobservable. A carpenter at the end of the day can actually *see* what he has built, a doctor can observe a patient responding to treatment, but a teacher oftentimes has to go along for months with relatively few noticeable results and, what is worse, with practically no recognition of his efforts. He can slave or merely mark time, develop his pupils or bore them, and at the end of the year he gets the same raise as anyone else.

Another discouraging phase of public education (or possibly "confusing" is the better term) is the multiplicity of aims or goals the teacher must strive for. When planning a period's work, you must ask yourself whether it is adapted to the individual pupil, whether it will aid in developing right attitudes, whether it will be appealing, and then you wonder whether you aren't wrong for insisting that the pupil learn something he or she isn't mature enough to see the need for. At the same time, the student must be trained to be polite, to have good social attitudes, to be a good citizen, to be prepared to take a rightful place in the world, to work with others and yet have independent views, to conform to the silly little disciplinary rules you must perforce set up and yet be ready to aid in reforming the future

world he or she must live in. You are strict and the
pupil's emotional development is harmed. You are
lenient and the pupils get out of control, making impossible the attainment of the above-listed objec-
tives. O teacher, how manifold are thy works!

But Freud or no Freud, the new teacher must have
discipline. I know you, for one, won't lie awake
nights wondering whether your dear little cherubs
are home on their downy couches with their little
negligent "censors" letting all kinds of repressed ideas
slip by to disturb them in symbolic dreams. So
get good discipline right away, and you will have
little trouble. If not, God help you! That's a plati-
tude, of course, and I needn't have mentioned it. But
the following suggestions may help:

1. Be consistent. Pupils soon learn how much they
can get away with and will be careful not to ex-
ceed the limit.
2. Set up a few classroom habits, such as a method
of calling to order, taking seats, passing papers,
leaving seats, reciting, etc. It doesn't matter much
just what you tell them to do as long as they know
exactly how they are to do it.
3. When punishing, don't act resentful. Do it calmly,
sometimes even with a smile, and help them see
that it is absolutely fair.
4. Some say a teacher should never let the pupil
know that he is angry. I think, however, that if
the situation warrants it, a good demonstration of
righteous indignation is very impressive. But it
soon loses its effect if done often, of course.
5. Don't talk too much. Get the pupils to realize that

you speak only when you have something important to say.
6. Repeat on item 1. The most important and by far the hardest. Just remember the rule someday about the fifth period when you have a cold or are sleepy.

Here are a few unorganized, haphazard suggestions that come to mind:

1. Don't get *too* friendly with pupils. They misinterpret your attitude and are inclined to take advantage of it.
2. Be careful of your voice. It's easy to become a comparative monotone and lull the pupils to a pleasant lassitude.
3. Keep your sense of humor. If necessary, *look* for something to laugh at. Just watching a group of kids at work or coming down the hall is usually sufficient.
4. Don't take teaching too seriously. Don't let those beautifully sweet and inspiring editorials in the education journals get you. Cultivate other interests. Teachers are the worst shop-talkers in the world. And, incidentally, poorer teachers as a result.
5. Above all, let your memory run back to your own eighth-grade experience, sitting in the front row with me, leading Miss Steigerwalt a merry chase. That's a wonderful antidote when you begin despairing for the coming generation.

I guess I don't need to say that teaching is a unique profession. It has its periods of elation and depression. Some days you will wonder how you stand it. Other days you will feel there is nothing so satisfying. Monday, you will be full of enthusiasm and plans for the future. Friday, you will look back and wonder just what you have accomplished. One period you will consider yourself a born teacher. Next period you will bewail the fate that gave you such a job. Wednesday, you will discover that John Jones has finally learned how to divide fractions. Thursday, he will seem to have forgotten everything. One week you will feel that the superintendent thinks you are the best teacher on the faculty. The next week you will be sure he is looking for an excuse to fire you. One month you will decide that at last you have arrived at a satisfactory philosophy of education. The next month you will look at the pupils coming into the room and wonder, What is it all for? Some days will be a month in passing. Some months will be a day in passing.

But, when the end of the year has arrived, the innumerable reports made out, good-byes said to your pupils and fellow teachers, and you are looking forward to an enjoyable summer vacation, you will smile at your mistakes, be amused at your doubts, be content with your appointed task, and once again be full of plans and enthusiasms for the next year.

Comme toujours,
Albert

P. S. By the way, the ideal disciplinarian as described above is largely the way I'd *like to be*, not the way I *am!*

Albert Thompson was a high school teacher in Pennsylvania, over fifty years ago, when he wrote the above letter of advice to a boyhood friend who had been newly appointed to a teaching job. Thompson eventually earned a doctorate and became a professor of education at Teachers College, Columbia University.

CHAPTER 21

The Accidental Teacher

*

Katherine Schulten

There was no way I was going to become a teacher. As an English major in college, I was often asked if I planned to teach. "Definitely not," I always said. I thought of teaching then the way most of the country probably still does—stressful, thankless, underpaid work with little room for advancement.

But then I found myself working with teenagers the summer after college and the experience was more interesting, more fun, than anything I'd done before. Since then I've taught the English language to Japanese businessman in Tokyo, I've counseled emotionally disturbed children in a Brooklyn junior high school, and now I teach English in a high school in Brooklyn. And all those experiences have reinforced my sense that teaching is the best, the most interesting job I could possibly have.

This year I'm in school myself getting a master's degree, but I'm also eager to be back in Room 210C teaching American literature. I laughed all day when I was teaching. I felt more alive than ever before or since, because I was using all the energy and creativity I had in work I loved. Reading literature and discussing it with kids, talking, laughing, inventing things—what could be better? For a year I worked in a publishing company, and the only thing anyone there ever said to anyone else was, "Could I borrow your stapler?" In the classroom there's always something interesting happening. Mike and Ludmilla are arguing about whether rhyme is essential to a poem; Ellie reads out loud her story called "The Worst Date" about going to a Bon Jovi concert with a boy who came to pick her up wearing a shirt made entirely out of metal chains. And Vilaire has made something called *The Scarlet Letter* Sin Game that he wants everyone to play. You have to twirl the spinner and advance around a board to pick up cards that say something like, "Chillingworth wants to become your friend. Go back two spaces."

I don't want to pretend my first year of teaching wasn't hard. It was. It's just that it was worth it, and the second year was a hundred times better. But I have to admit that I spent three or four hours a night planning lessons and grading papers that first year and that I used to have a sick feeling in the pit of my stomach every single morning on the way to school wondering if my writing lesson would go well or if Craig was going to get in a fight with Michael as he usually did. I cried once in my principal's office after he observed a lesson that didn't work. In my first semester I had a class that was so unruly that my chairman finally suggested I simply refuse to teach any more lessons; I was to put assignments up on the board for them to do silently in their seats. Fortunately I never had to resort to that, but many nights I had nightmares that featured at least one member of that class.

But, on the other hand, there's the day that Rebecca, who hardly ever spoke, stood up in class and sang a Puerto Rican lullaby her mother used to sing to her. It was so beautiful we all just sat there for a few minutes before we could respond. And there's the time three of my students made up and performed for the class a rap song for *The Grapes of Wrath*. It began, "The Joads were a family/innocent and naïve/The bank said get off/so their land they had to leave," and featured scratching by David on a 1960s record player borrowed from the library, and a chorus that went, "We be readin', We be readin'."

Or there's coming into school every morning and feeling like a celebrity because fifty different kids say to you, "Hi, Ms. Schulten" before you can even get to your office. Or the time that Mark brought a pair of his tube socks to school for me to wear because I had a cold and he worried that I wasn't warm enough just wearing stockings. Or at the end of my first semester when I was still a nervous wreck about teaching and Jessica wrote at the bottom of her final paper, "I think you are one of the best teachers in this school. Thank you for making our class so fun." Or the time we were laughing so hard in fifth period that a student from the classroom next door had to come in and ask us to be quiet.

The first time I was ever alone in a room with thirty-four high school students I nearly panicked. They sat in their seats waiting for me to say something, tell them to do something, and I wanted to run out of the room and tell the Board of Education they'd made a big mistake. And I grew to accept the fact that I couldn't create a separate "teacher self" to become at 8:30 and leave at 2:30, especially when I'd be out running in the park later in the evening and I'd hear, "Yo, Ms. Schulten" and some kid from fourth period would shoot by on his bike. The next day in school I'd be trying to say something intelligent about *The Scarlet Letter* and I'd have to hear, "Ms. Schulten, Joe says he saw you jogging in the park yesterday. I hear you jog pretty slow."

I took Spanish class with the sophomores last year. I was going to Mexico for the summer, and I wanted a way to get some speaking practice before I got there. I sat next to Sean, one of the students in my fifth-period class, and behind Jason, who had failed at midterm, in a tiny desk with gum under it and Spanish verb conjugations written all over it by former students cheating on their tests. The kids in the class got to call me Katerina instead of Ms. Schulten, and I had to do all the homework every night. Sean and Jason were always trying to arrange a trade with me—I could copy their Spanish homework if I'd let them out of doing one essay for English. It was tempting, but I resisted.

Then came the final exam. I had studied for it for two days and finished the test twenty minutes before anyone else in the class; I knew I'd done well. But then the teacher, who was obsessed with baseball, said, "Anyone who can name five Spanish baseball players will get ten extra points," and I got mad. Even though I'd probably made a hundred on the test anyway, I suddenly got a student's viewpoint with a vengeance. If you didn't know anything about baseball, suddenly you couldn't get ten extra points? "That isn't fair"—the age-old student cry—passed through my mind. The boy in front of me was writing like crazy—José Canseco, Sid Fernandez, Raphael Santana—and I found myself compulsively looking at what he was writing. It was at this moment, of course, that Jason looked over at me and yelled out, "Hey, Ms. Schulten's cheating!"

I had to hear it in the halls for the next three days. "Ms. Schulten, I heard you cheated on your Spanish test." Even the principal asked me, jokingly—I think— if it was true. What could I say? That experience taught me that I'd better do my best at all times to remember what sitting in the little seat, not the big desk, feels like.

The people who graduated from college with me all have jobs in offices in Manhattan and Boston and Philadelphia. It's hard for me to imagine what they do all day. They talk about watching the clock and living for weekends. I live for weekdays. When I'm in school, I'm completely absorbed and have to remind myself at the end of the school day of the details of my personal life. The things you can think about during the day while you're teaching are some of the most engaging things there are: How can I make this poem I love interesting to other people? How can I get Michael in the back of the room more involved? How can I help Ellie feel better when I know she's having real problems at home?

I was amazed at the end of my first semester of teaching to realize that I'd learned more about literature and about learning than I'd ever learned when I was a student. I don't think I really knew how to read books until I learned how to teach them. And I don't think I understood how to be fair and consistent and loving in my relationships until I had to learn how to do it in dealing with kids. I fell into teaching accidentally, but it's possible that I've been happier in the classroom than I've ever been anywhere else. I think I'll be there for a long time—and not by accident.

Katherine Schulten is now in her fifth year of teaching at a high school in Brooklyn, New York, which provides the setting for her story.

CHAPTER 22

The Green Monongahela

*

John Taylor Gatto

In the beginning I became a teacher without realizing it. At the time I was growing up on the banks of the green Monongahela River forty miles southwest of Pittsburgh, and on the banks of that deep green and always mysterious river I became a student, too, master of the flight patterns of blue dragonflies and cunning adversary of the iridescent ticks that infested the riverbank willows.

"Mind you watch the ticks, Jackie!" Grandmother Mossie would call as I headed for the riverbank, summer and winter, only a two-minute walk across the trolley tracks of Main Street and the Pennsylvania Railroad tracks that paralleled them. I watched the red and yellow beetles chewing holes in the pale green leaves as I ran to the riverbank. It was on the river that I drank my first beer, smoked every cigarette brand obtainable, and watched dangerous men and women make love there at night on blankets—all before I was twelve. It was my laboratory: there I learned to watch closely and draw conclusions.

But how did the river make me a teacher? Listen. It was alive with paddle-wheel steamers in center channel, the turning paddles churning up clouds of white spray, making the green river boil bright orange where its chemical undercurrent was troubled; from shore you could clearly hear the loud THUMP, THUMP, THUMP on the water. From all over town young boys ran to gaze in awe. A dozen times a day. No one ever became indifferent to the riverboats because nothing important can ever really be boring. You see the difference, don't you? There are no comparisons between those serious boats and the truly boring spacecraft of the past few decades, junk in orbit without a purpose a boy can believe in; it's hard to even pretend an interest in satellites, now that I teach for a living and would like to pretend for the sake of the New York kids who won't have paddle-wheelers in their lives. The rockets are dull toys that children put aside the day after Christmas, never to touch again; the riverboats were serious magic, clearly demarcating the world of boys from the world of men. Levi-Strauss would know how to explain.

In Monongahela, by that river, everyone was my teacher. Daily one of the three-mile-long trains would stop in town to take on water and coal; then the brakeman and engineer would step among the snot-nosed kids and spin railroad yarns, let us run in and out of boxcars, over and under flatcars, tank cars, coal cars, and an endless number of other specialty cars whose function we memorized as easily as enemy plane silhouettes. Once a year maybe we got taken into the caboose that reeked of stale beer and were offered a bologna on white bread sandwich. The anonymous men lectured, advised, and inspired the boys of Monongahela—it was as much their job as operating the trains.

When a riverboat was short of supplies it hove-to in midchannel, discharging a boat crew who rowed to shore, tying their skiff to one of the willows. That was the excuse for every rickety skiff in the twelve-block-long town to fill up with kids, pulling like Vikings, sometimes with sticks instead of oars, to raid *Belle of Pittsburgh* or the *Original River Queen*. Some kind of natural etiquette was at work in Monongahela. The rules didn't need to be written down—if men had time they showed boys how to grow up. We didn't whine when the time was up. Men had work to do—we understood that and scampered away grateful for the flash of our own futures they had time to reveal, however small it was.

I was arrested three times growing up in Mononga-hela, or rather picked up by the police and taken to jail to await a visit from Pappy to spring me. I wouldn't trade those times for anything. The first time I was nine, caught on my belly under a parked car at night half an hour after curfew; in 1943 blinds were always drawn in the Mon Valley for fear Hitler's planes would somehow find a way to reach across the Atlantic to our eighty miles of steel mills lining both banks of the river. The Nazis were apparently waiting for a worried mother to go searching for her son with a flashlight after curfew, then WHAMO! Down would descend the Teutonic airfleet!

Charlie was the cop's name. Down to the lockup we went—no call to Mother until Charlie diagrammed the deadly menace of Goering's Luftwaffe. What a geopolitics lesson that was! Another time I speared a goldfish in the town fishpond and was brought from jail to the library where I was sentenced to read for a month about the lives of animals. Finally, on VJ Day when the Japanese cried uncle, I accepted a dare and broke the window of the police cruiser with a slingshot. Confessing, I suffered my first encounter with employment to pay for the glass, becoming sweep-up boy in my grandfather's printing office at fifty cents a week.

After I went away to Cornell I saw Monongahela and its green river only one more time. My family moved again and again and again, but in my own heart I never left Monongahela, where I learned to teach from being taught by everyone in town, where I learned to work from being asked to shoulder my share of responsibility even as a boy, and where I learned to find adventures I made myself from the everyday stuff around me—the river and the people who lived alongside it.

In 1964, $18,000 was a lot of money. That's what I walked away from to become a teacher. I had been a copywriter on the fast track of advertising, a young fellow with a knack for writing thirty-second television commercials. My work required about one full day a month to complete, the rest of the time being spent in power breakfasts, after-work martinis at Michael's Pub, keeping up with the shifting fortunes of about twenty agencies in order to gauge the right time to jump ship for more money, and endless parties that always seemed to culminate in a colossal headache.

It bothered me that all the urgencies of the job were generated externally, but it bothered me more that the work I was doing seemed to have very little importance—even to the people who were paying for it. Worst of all, the problems the work posed were cut from such a narrow spectrum that it was clear that past, present, and future were to be of a piece: a twenty-nine-year-old man's work was no different from a thirty-nine-year-old man's work or a forty-nine-year-old man's work, though there didn't seem to *be* any forty-nine-year-old copywriters (I had no idea why not).

"I'm leaving," I said one day to the copy chief.

"Are you nuts, Jack? You'll get profit-sharing this year. We can match any offer you've got. Leaving for who?"

"For nobody, Dan. I mean I'm going to teach school."

"When you see your mother next, tell her for me she raised a moron. Christ! Are *you* going to be sorry! In New York City we don't have schools; we have holding pens for lost souls. Teaching is a scam, a welfare project for losers who can't do anything else!"

Round and round I went with my advertising colleagues for a few days. Their scorn only firmed my resolve; the riverboats and trains of Monongahela were working inside me. I needed something to do that wasn't absurd more than I needed another party or a new abstract number in my bankbook.

And so I became a junior high school substitute teacher, working the beat from what's now Lincoln Center to Columbia, my alma mater, and from Harlem to the South Bronx. After three months on the job, the dismal working conditions, ugly rooms, torn books, repeated instances of petty complaints from authorities, the bells, buzzers, drab teacher food in the cafeterias, unpressed clothing, the inexplicable absence of conversation about children on the part of teachers . . . had just about done me in.

In fact, on the very first day I taught I was attacked by a boy waving a chair above his head. It happened in an infamous junior high school on 113th Street. I was given the eighth-grade typing class—seventy-five students and typewriters—with this one injunction: "Under no circumstances are you to allow them to type. You lack the proper license. Is that understood?"

It couldn't have taken more than sixty seconds after I closed the door and issued the order not to type before 150 hands snaked under the typewriter covers and began to type. But not all at once—that would have been too easy. First, three machines began to CLACK, CLACK from the right rear. Quick, who were the culprits? I would race to that corner screaming STOP! when suddenly from behind my back three other machines would begin. Whirling about, I caught one small boy in the act. Then, to a veritable symphony of machines clicking, bells ringing, platens being thrown, I hoisted the boy from his chair and announced at the top of my foolish lungs I would make an example of this miscreant.

"Look out!" a girl shouted, and I turned toward her voice just in time to see a large brother of the little fellow I held heading toward me with a chair raised above his head. Releasing his brother, I seized a chair myself and raised it aloft. A standoff! We regarded each other at a distance of about ten feet for what seemed forever, the class jeering and howling, when the room door opened and the assistant principal, the very man who'd given the no-typing order, appeared.

"Mr. Gatto, have these children been typing?"

"No sir," I said, lowering my chair, "but I think they want to. What do you suggest they do instead?"

He looked at me for signs of impudence or insubordination for a second, then as if thinking better of rebuking this upstart he said merely, "Fall back on your reserves," and left the room.

Most of the kids laughed—they'd seen this drama enacted before.

The situation was defused, but silently I dubbed this place "The Death School" and, stopping by the school office on my way home, I told the secretary not to call me again if they needed a sub.

The very next morning my phone rang at six-thirty. "Are you available for work today, Mr. Gatto?" said the voice briskly.

"Who is this?" I asked suspiciously. (Ten schools were using me for sub work in those days, and each generally identified itself at once.)

"The law clearly states, Mr. Gatto, that we do not have to tell you who we are until you tell us whether you are available for work."

"Never mind!" I bellowed. "There's only one school that would pull such crap! The answer is NO! I am never available to work in your pigpen school!" And I slammed the receiver back into its cradle.

The truth was that none of the sub assignments were boat rides; schools had an uncanny habit of exploiting substitutes and providing seemingly little support for their survival. It's likely that I'd have returned to advertising if a little girl, desperate to free herself from an intolerable situation, hadn't drawn me into her personal nightmare and shown me how I could find my own significance in teaching—just as those strong men in the riverboats and trains had found their own significance, a currency all of us need to buy self-esteem.

It happened this way. Occasionally I'd get a call from an elementary school. This particular day it was a third-grade assignment at a school in Spanish Harlem, which in those days was nearly 100 percent Hispanic in its student body and 100 percent non-Hispanic in its teaching staff.

Like many desperate teachers, I killed most of the day listening to the kids read, one after another and expending most of my energy trying to shut the audience up. This class had a very low ranking, and no one was able to put more than three or four words together without stumbling. All of a sudden, though, a little girl named Milagros sailed through a selection without a mistake. After class I called her over to my desk and asked why she was in this class of bad readers. She replied that they (the administration) wouldn't let her out because, as they explained to her mother, she was really a bad reader who had fantasies of being a better reader than she was. "But look, Mr. Gatto, my brother is in the sixth grade, and I can read every word in his English book better than he can!"

I was a little intrigued, but truthfully not much. Surely the school authorities knew what they were doing. Still, the little girl seemed so frustrated I invited her to calm down and read to me from the sixth-grade book. I explained that if she did well, I would take her case to the principal. I expected nothing.

Milagros, on the other hand, expected justice. Diving into *The Devil and Daniel Webster*, she polished off the first two pages without a gulp. My God, I thought, this is a real reader. What is she doing here? Well, maybe it was a simple accident, easily corrected. I sent her home, promising to argue her case. Little did I suspect what a hornet's nest my request to have Milagros moved to a better class would cause.

"You have some nerve, Mr. Gatto. I can't remember

when a substitute ever told me how to run my school before. Have you taken specialized courses in reading?"

"No."

"Well then, suppose you leave these matters to the experts!"

"But this kid can *read*!" I insisted.

"What do you suggest?"

"I suggest you test her, and if she isn't a dummy, get her out of the class she's in!"

"I don't like your tone. None of our children are dummies, Mr. Gatto. And you will find that girls like Milagros have many ways to fool amateurs like yourself. This is a matter of a child having memorized one story. You can see if I had to waste my time arguing with people like you I'd have no time left to run a school."

But, strangely, I felt self-appointed as the girl's champion, even though I'd probably never see her again. The principal finally agreed to test Milagros herself the following Wednesday after school. I made it a point to tell the little girl the next day. By that time I'd come to consider the principal was probably right—she'd memorized one story—but still I warned her she'd need to know the vocabulary from the whole advanced reader and be able to read any story the principal picked without hesitation. My responsibility was over, I told myself.

The following Wednesday after school I waited in the room for Milagros's ordeal to be over. At three-thirty she shyly opened the door of the room.

"How'd it go?" I asked.

"I don't know," she answered, "but I didn't make any mistakes. The principal was very angry, I could tell."

I saw the principal early next morning before school

opened. "It seems we did make a mistake with Milagros," she admitted curtly. "She will be transferred, Mr. Gatto. Her mother has been informed."

Several weeks later when I got back to the school to sub, Milagros dropped by, telling me she was in "the fast class" now and doing very well. She also gave me a sealed card. When I got home that night, I found it, unopened, in my suitcoat pocket. I opened it and saw a gaudy birthday card with blue flowers on it. Opening the card, I read, "A teacher like you cannot be found. Signed, Your student, Milagros."

That simple sentence made me a teacher for life. It was the first praise I'd ever heard in my working existence that had any meaning. I never forgot it, though I never saw Milagros again or even heard of her until twenty-four years later. Then one day I picked up a newspaper and read that Mireya Guzman had won the Distinguished Occupational Teacher Award of the State Education Department for "demonstrated achievement and exemplary professionalism." The article also noted that a secretarial studies teacher in New York City had been selected as a Manhattan Teacher of the Year and nominated by the National Council for Women for their prestigious annual award.

Ah, Mireya, is it just possible that I was your Monongahela River? No matter, a teacher like you cannot be found.

John Taylor Gatto began his teaching career twenty-five years ago in New York City. He currently teaches at a junior high school in New York and was selected New York City Teacher of the Year in 1990.

CHAPTER 23

My Ambition: To Teach

*

Yetta Haber Farber

"You are too smart to be a teacher" were the words scrawled across the top of my essay entitled "My Ambition: To Teach." I was just eleven years old and in the sixth grade.

I graduated from Cornell University as a premed student. I wanted to be a pediatrician, so I took courses during summers in child development and education at Cornell and at Columbia University. Then I planned to teach school for just one year before applying to medical school.

The year was 1950. I was assigned to a school in one of the poorest sections of Brooklyn. "How can you work there?" "It's such a bad neighborhood!" "There are drugs and shootings there." Such comments by well-meaning friends frightened me, but my excitement at being a classroom teacher overpowered their warnings, and I arrived at my kindergarten class full of idealism and enthusiasm.

On the first day of school, as a never-ending line

of kindergarten children marched into my classroom, I counted forty-five children, mostly black, a few white, and two Asian-American. "Don't worry," said the principal, "there are two teachers assigned to this classroom." The second teacher never came.

I had not prepared activities for such a large group. To gain control of the children, I led them in a lively and long John Philip Sousa march. Suddenly one of the doors to my room opened, and a first-grade teacher and her class paraded through my room on the way to the bathroom. I could not believe I would have this disruption every day. Soon a second-grade teacher and her students similarly trailed through my room on the way to the bathroom. I worried about my children joining these bathroom lines that went through my room several times a day. I counted and recounted my children all day long.

The help that I desperately needed came as a result of my expression of frustration in the teachers' lunch room. A young teacher of mentally retarded children offered to send me two of her most capable older children to help my children take off their jackets every morning. Fifth- and sixth-grade teachers sent me children who had finished their classroom work, and they, too, helped me with my classroom projects.

Another of my helpers was Marilyn's father. Marilyn was a quiet, pretty black child with hair smelling of castile soap and with sweet-smelling powder sprinkled on her neck. Her father was a mailman who worked in the neighborhood. He came to pick up Marilyn every day about fifteen minutes before school was over because he did not want her walking alone in that neighborhood. His early arrival proved to be a help for me because he used that time helping to dress other children.

Every Thursday I pinned notes on the children reminding parents that on Friday morning we would have a program with their children singing and reciting nursery rhymes, marching, and acting out stories. I decorated the children with crepe paper bows, sashes, and streamers. At these programs I got to know the parents and their difficult lives. I came to understand the problems of the children.

Joey came to school every day wearing a football helmet to protect his head. Joey's mother explained that she and Joey's stepfather had had an argument and "to get even with her" he had dangled Joey out a third-story window, holding him by one leg. The mother had tried to grab Joey's arm during this fracas. The father let go and the mother felt Joey slipping. He fell and fractured his skull. After a long hospital stay he was allowed to come to school—in the helmet. Everyone made fun of Joey until I bought another helmet and let other children wear it as a reward for being good. Joey was accepted after that.

Troy, a foster child who had lived with three previous foster parents, now had a very caring foster mother. Each day, as soon as Troy entered the classroom, he went to the window, looked out, and asked, "Teacha, is it dark outside yet? Is it dark outside?" He wouldn't leave the window to play or for snacks. He was afraid it would get dark and no one would be there to pick him up. I told Troy I would watch the window if he joined the others to play. He came to the window less and less each day.

Mary was a slight, blond child. Her matted hair framed a pretty face. On her first day of school, when many of the children were wearing new clothing, she wore an old dress about three sizes too large. The sleeves on her sweater were so long they had to be rolled up three or four times. She was very shy. She bit her nails and her lips until they were sore. The children didn't include her in their play. I sent a note to Mary's mother, asking her to shorten her dress so that she could join in the play without stumbling over it (it hung almost to the floor). There was no response. I shortened the dress myself and obtained some clothing in her size. Almost immediately she was better accepted by the other children. By the end of the year she was a much happier child—no nail biting, no lip biting.

I kept my eye on these three children, as well as on the many others who came to school with problems. I made sure they got an extra cookie, an extra hug, and an extra turn being "leader." For most of the children, being in school was the happiest time—away from the problems of home and neighborhood. They learned to count, say the alphabet, sing, and dance. Their joy made school a happy place for me. So I remained there.

Why did I continue to teach in this urban school under such poor conditions? How could I endure classes that were too large, with poor equipment, few supplies, bathroom lines passing through my class every day, the bad neighborhood? The answer was fairly simple: I felt very needed. I felt I had a positive influence on children who desperately needed someone who cared what happened to them. I wanted to give them a good experience every day to try to compensate for their poor environment and bad experiences. I wanted them to know that they could be curious, explore, ask questions, and make mistakes. I wanted learning to be fun and not a chore. Despite what my sixth-grade teacher had said,

I found teaching took every bit of intelligence I could muster.

In short, I had fallen in love with teaching and taught for thirty-five years. I decided not to be a pediatrician, but nonetheless I became a healer of children—a teacher.

Yetta Haber Farber began her teaching career in Brooklyn, New York. She is now retired, but continues to teach as a volunteer at an elementary school in Paterson, New Jersey, and works as a tutor.

CHAPTER 24

Graduation

*

Ron Wolfson

The desks were piled in a pyramid, the chalkboard eraser had been thrown out of the eighth-floor window, and Hector, a mountainous ninth grader, was dangling Roman, an undersized child, upside down by his ankles. Luis rushed at me to complain that Danny locked his bookbag in a locker. (Luis and Danny were the two best students in this class.) When I reached my desk a dozen children surrounded me to describe the unexpected event that kept them, once again, from completing an assignment. Others began to ask for special privileges, but before I could give the bathroom pass to any of the six who swore they were at the point of spontaneous release, I asked Hector, gently, to put Roman down. The usual chaos was in place.

Hector is an interesting example. After attending the first few days of class, he disappeared for eight weeks, only to return with wedding pictures and a message that I must pass him. He was typical of my special class of ninth-grade kids, all diagnosed as "slow learners," a phrase that can denote any condition from emotionally disturbed to hyperactive to mildly retarded. Others might describe Hector as simply a big kid who didn't care for school.

In my special class, attendance was sporadic, homework rarely done, tardiness the norm, cheating occurred for the sport of it, and verbal sparring between students took up large chunks of class time. On three occasions fistfights started with little warning. This ninth-grade class was my introduction to teaching.

Even in December the sun made the classroom unbearably hot, and the students moved their desks into a large square along the sides of the classroom. They had broken all the blinds, for no particular reason than to see if they could get away with it, and now they realized that the room was too bright. Their inability to understand the relationship between cause and effect (or an inability to realize the relationship before it's too late) accounted for much of their behavior.

Although the program for Hector and my other ninth graders was the school's sincere attempt to meet the needs of particular students, in many ways it represented what was wrong with the school system. The students were placed together all day, assigned to a nine-period schedule designed to keep them busy, and were given a clear impression that nothing was really expected of them. This year they were unloaded on a brand-new teacher, me, with no experience and with a new curriculum that seemed nearly impossible to cover even under favorable circumstances. There was no textbook and the only aid I was given was a book of lesson plans from the mid-1960s, which besides being hopelessly out of date was for students with greater skills than those of my kids, few of whom were expected to graduate from high school.

As a group, my special ninth-grade class was destructive, rude, uncontrollable, immature, undisciplined, discourteous, cruel, disrespectful, and obnoxious. Some students were nearly illiterate. Yet, taken as individuals, they were not bad kids. At the end of one afternoon, a full session of thumbtacks on students' seats, constant bickering, weird gaseous noises, and "Mr. Wooooooolfson" calls every time I turned my back, one student asked with utter sincerity, "But you still like us, don't you?" They were, in the end, children, and they needed approval and affection as do all children.

While these special students are an extreme example, my other classes were only slightly less of a struggle. Every day witnessed the same battles: getting kids to class, beseeching them to come on time, repeatedly asking for quiet, insisting that they take out their notebooks, reminding them to pay attention, imploring them to participate, helping them to understand, persuading them to do homework, encouraging them to study, convincing them that there is something worthwhile in learning about American government or global studies. A totally exhausting experience that first year, teaching usually left me fast asleep before ten o'clock on Friday nights, my reward for making it through another week.

All of what I've just described is true, and nothing I could say would make it not be true. And yet, it is still possible to choose other moments that year that could give a very different impression. Let me make the contrast as stark as possible and choose graduation, a joyous celebration of achievement, a necessary symbol for stu-

dent and teacher alike. Graduation, in the end, show
that school is worth it. For students like mine, graduation was and is not only an awards ceremony, but also
a song session and a revival meeting. It is a ceremony
of energy and sentiment and spirit that comes at the
end of a long, arduous journey, an adventure not always
continued voluntarily, full of jagged climbs and twisting
falls like those of erasers chucked from eighth-floor windows, of unexpected starts and stops. Students wear
their finest suits and most beautiful dresses to graduation, because for many this is truly the most important
day of their lives. On this occasion, the youth and happiness of these students radiate and no one is immune
to their glow.

At our school's graduation ceremony, three girls gathered on the stage to sing solos from "The Greatest Love
of All," a song by Michael Masser and Linda Creed
that conveys the importance of building self-esteem in
children, all children.

The second soloist began to cry in the middle of her
part (indeed, not a single student speaker got through
a speech without shedding tears), and when it became
apparent she would not be able to continue, the entire
graduating class picked up the song at full volume.
They sang not to one another or to the audience but to
the heavens.

I believe the children are our future
Teach them well and let them lead the way
Show them all the beauty they possess inside
Give them a sense of pride to make it easier
Let the children's laughter remind us of what we
used to be.

The greatest love of all
is easy to achieve.
Learning to love yourself
is the greatest love of all.

At the end of the ceremony the students half sang, half cried a song simply called "Farewell." Students held on to each other, hugged each other, cried on each other, male and female, female and female, male and male. They had made it, some against impossibly long odds.

I am not fooling myself into thinking that all the graduating students deserved high school diplomas or that even half of them have the necessary reading and writing skills to make their way through life. I can only wonder helplessly about the futures of teenagers whose only understanding of academic achievement comes from their own inadequate schooling. What was revealed at graduation, though, was an emotional togetherness and sensitivity rarely displayed in the classroom. It was a wonderful way to remember that first year.

In another commencement ceremony that year, at the school where I did my student teaching, the salutatorian of the graduating class told of how his father, a Greek immigrant, worked sixteen-hour days so that his son could have a better life. The Harvard-bound valedictorian, who had come to this country from Puerto Rico four years ago, told his fellow Hispanics that they have the worst drop-out rate in New York City, that they must work to do better in school. The two speakers, tassels swinging from mortarboards, were cheered lustily; on this one day at least everyone believed in the American Dream.

Then the entire class sang "Man in the Mirror," a

song about making the world a better place. It woul take a really hard heart not to be moved by the sight of the students standing as one, arms in the air, swaying back and forth, singing this song with conviction.

After the ceremony, everyone gathered outside the theater where the ceremony had been held. I ran into a few of my students. Some introduced me to parents, others gave me a hug or a kiss, some took my picture. I looked at these children, and I thought of how they had made me laugh and made me angry and made me curse. But above all I was happy for them: their graduation meant more to me than any of my own. In some ways we had been through a similar journey, viewing life from the ground-floor level of the urban classroom, a bit wiser now for the experience. I watched them smile joyously at their own accomplishments, sufficiently warmed for having, in some minor way, shared in them. I was neither a hero nor a fool. I was an observer, both puzzled and delighted by what I saw. I realized that the equation of effort to results, of positives to negatives, while never properly balanced, could still tilt just far enough toward satisfying to make teaching worthwhile.

Ron Wolfson started his teaching career at a high school in the Bronx, four years ago. He is currently teaching in Brooklyn, New York.

CHAPTER 25

Memories Are Made of This

✳

Roberta Vicki Sherman

If you're lucky, there's at least one class in your teaching career in which the chemistry between you and the children produces a special bond. For me it was 1964, my first year of teaching. So when I received a message at school that said I should call Mark F—— at such and such a number, I was at first quite surprised, but, on reflection, less so. He was one of the boys in my fourth-grade class that year, the first class that had become for me such a cherished memory.

Before I called Mark, I pulled out my picture of that year's class. I found Mark in it and saw how accurate the mental image I had of him was. What did he look like now? What did they all look like, now that they were thirty-three or thirty-four? What challenges did my grown-up children now face in their careers? Which ones were married? Which ones were parents? Were they as curious about life and as responsive to it as they had been then? Did they remember me? Attached to the photo were some yellowing sheets of paper, notes

I had made for myself that first year. I read them over slowly and with yearning. Then I called Mark.

"Hello, Miss Sherman, is that really you?" came the deep voice on the other end of the phone.

"Yes, it's me. How are you, cutie?"

With an audible sigh in his voice Mark said, "You sound the same as then."

We chatted for a while, reminiscing. He told me he and two other boys from my class, Steven and Mitchell, had remained friends. Then Mark grew excited as he went on to say they wanted to take me to dinner and go over old times. We made a date for the coming Saturday.

"I'm going to bring my fourth-grade report card for you to see." Mark laughed. "Steven's got his, too. We never forgot you."

I was very touched. He proceeded to tell me they'd pick me up and we'd go on from there. As I hung up, I felt great excitement at anticipating the coming reunion. On many occasions over the years I've wondered what became of "my children." Now, I would in some small part find out.

Anticipating the reunion made me really begin to remember getting my first job and teaching that first and well-remembered class. It was either great good luck or an absolutely fated part of my destiny that I ended up at the school where I myself had attended kindergarten to sixth grade. In the back of my mind I'd always hoped to teach there someday. As a recent college graduate, I was awaiting word in early September from one of eleven schools I'd applied to when I had a sudden phone call from my aunt. She informed me that she'd heard from the president of the Parents Association that a vacancy existed at my old school. "Get to the Bronx immediately," she commanded. I was happy to follow her instructions.

All went well from there. I was hired on the spot. With a smile the principal shook my hand, wished me well, said the necessary papers would be sent that day, and showed me out of the office. The whole thing—in and out—took less than half an hour. Now I was officially a teacher, and a teacher in a school where I'd dreamed of being. I couldn't wait to actually get into the classroom!

Although I was very eager to put my ideas and the teaching techniques I'd learned to work, I was also frightened. Could I make learning both interesting and informative? Could I help my children come to care about learning? I tried to relax and concentrate on the positive. I began work on my lesson plans for the first day. I planned—and overplanned—to ensure enough diversity in the day's work.

The next morning found me, plans in hand, at school at eight o'clock. I picked up my keys and counted the 102 steps up to Room 504. "An added plus," I mused, "I'll be able to lose twenty pounds by Christmas." Then I opened the door to my new world.

What a letdown! The room was painted a horrible shade of green. Chairs were stacked on movable desks piled in the middle of the room. Yellow paint was peeling off various mismatched bulletin boards. I plopped down in the wooden teacher's chair. I breathed deeply a few times, then I jumped up and began arranging all the chairs and desks. After that I began visualizing what my bulletin boards would look like with children's work adorning them. I found large sheets of colored paper in the closet and a stapler in the top drawer of the teacher's desk. I began covering up the seedy-looking bulletin boards. I was interrupted by the sound of a bell. I froze! They're on their way up. Get those plans out of your bag.

The children entered silently, eyeing me as they walked. I looked them over, too. When everyone was seated, I put my name on the board and plunged right in. The morning was a success. Everything went better than planned. Presumably, the afternoon would go well, too. Wrong! In the middle of the science lesson, children at the back of the room came running forward, screeching, holding their noses. Left behind was a frail-looking girl with tears running down onto her dress. Beneath her seat on the floor was the embarrassing evidence. She had had an attack of diarrhea.

Fighting against the ensuing chaos, I calmed everyone down, sent for the custodial helper, cooed at and petted the little girl, dispatched her to the main office with her home telephone number and a note, and spoke to the rest of the class about how embarrassing such an accident must have been to the girl, asking them to place themselves in her position. How would they have felt if this had happened to them? I finished the science lesson and ended on what I hoped was a high note. I was now officially initiated.

The first year was difficult but rewarding. I especially remember the first Parent-Teacher Conference Night in November. It was torture. Some parents couldn't believe how well their child was doing, others couldn't believe how poorly. During the first conference I saw a parent or parents of thirty-three children. In my yellowing notes about that first year I found a list of direct quotations of remarks parents made to me that night:

1. I can't understand it. He's not like this at home.
2. Are you sure that's my child you're talking about?
3. What can I do to help him? Isn't there something a little more drastic?
4. How can you tell I help her with her homework? . . . Oh!
5. Of course I don't beat him up if he doesn't get good marks. Wait till I get him at home for telling such stories!
6. We help him at home, but he's so stupid.
7. He told us you don't like him. Confidentially, we don't either.
8. He told you his brothers write his book reports?
9. You're lucky I'm here. This is usually my mah-jongg night.
10. I think that's cute. I used to be the same way in school.
11. You should have taught her brother. Such a bright boy!
12. You should get a medal for teaching my son. (This was Mark's mother.)
13. He's really getting something out of school this year. Thank you.

But if some parts of the year, like many of those parent conferences, were torture, others fully redeemed them. A few of us teachers wheeled and dealed with a movie theater manager and a coffeeshop owner. We succeeded in getting a special price for our classes early on a Sunday morning. Many a happy time was spent on the subway traveling to our special Sunday morning entertainment package.

Also delightful were the trips my students and I made after school exploring historic landmarks, museums, and the city in general. It was officially part of our social studies curriculum, a unit on Old New York, but the fun we had made it seem like something we'd begged to do. I also found time and money that year to initiate the custom of trips to the Christmas and the Easter shows at Radio City Music Hall with my most improved students. Those times were wonderful for me, and for them, too, I hope. . . .

Yes, I did go out with "my three men" on the appointed day. I saw what wonderful, sensitive, kind, gentle, loving men they'd become. I was picked up in a stretch limousine and toasted with champagne. We dined in Chinatown and went to Little Italy for coffee and more talk. I was presented with a solar-powered calculator in a brass holder. Engraved on the front was "Teacher of the Century—Miss Sherman." The boys' names appeared on the inside. We promised to stay in touch as we hugged and kissed goodbye.

That first year, that first class, was so special to me. If I had had my way, I'd never have promoted them. I'd have kept them forever.

Roberta Vicki Sherman has been teaching for over twenty-eight years, at the same elementary school in the Bronx, New York, that she herself attended as a child.

Index

*

169

PENGUIN PUTNAM INC.
Online

Your Internet gateway to a virtual environment with
hundreds of entertaining and enlightening books
from Penguin Putnam Inc.

While you're there, get the latest buzz on the best authors and books around—

Tom Clancy, Patricia Cornwell, W.E.B. Griffin,
Nora Roberts, William Gibson, Robin Cook,
Brian Jacques, Catherine Coulter, Stephen King,
Ken Follett, Terry McMillan, and many more!

**Penguin Putnam Online is located at
http://www.penguinputnam.com**

PENGUIN PUTNAM NEWS

Every month you'll get an inside look at our upcom-
ing books and new features on our site. This is an
ongoing effort to provide you with the most
up-to-date information about
our books and authors.

Subscribe to Penguin Putnam News at
http://www.penguinputnam.com/newsletters